THE ANGRY BOOK

THE ANGRY BOOK

Theodore Isaac Rubin, M.D.

COLLIER BOOKS
MACMILLAN PUBLISHING COMPANY
NEW YORK

MAXWELL MACMILLAN CANADA
TORONTO

MAXWELL MACMILLAN INTERNATIONAL
NEW YORK   OXFORD   SINGAPORE   SYDNEY

Collier Books
Macmillan Publishing Company
866 Third Avenue
New York, NY 10022

Maxwell Macmillan Canada, Inc.
1200 Eglinton Avenue East
Suite 200
Don Mills, Ontario M3C 3N1

Macmillan Publishing Company is part of the Maxwell Communication Group of Companies.

Library of Congress Cataloging-in-Publication Data

Rubin, Theodore Isaac.
The angry book / by Theodore Isaac Rubin.
-- 1st Collier Books Trade ed.
p. cm.
"Collier Books."
ISBN 0-02-036565-9
1. Anger.   I. Title.
BF575.A3R8   1993   93-7223   CIP
152.4'7–dc20

Macmillan books are available at special discounts for bulk purchases for sales promotions, premiums, fund-raising, or educational use. For details, contact:

Special Sales Director
Macmillan Publishing Company
866 Third Avenue
New York, NY 10022

First Collier Books Edition 1970

First Collier Books Trade Edition 1993

10   9   8   7   6

Printed in the United States of America

To Four of My Friends and Colleagues:

Jerome Fass, M.D.

Bella Van Bark, M.D.

Harvey Kaye, M.D.

Bernard Spector, M.D.

I am grateful to my former teachers, at the American Institute for Psychoanalysis, for my training in Karen Horney's theory.

Dr. Horney's theory lives on in her books and in the work we do. Without it, this book would not be possible.

CONTENTS

CONTENTS

CONTENTS

CONTENTS

INTRODUCTION

This book is about a basic human emotion—*anger*. Too often anger is not seen as basic or human. Anger is easily the most maligned and perverted of feelings and responses. Although there is an enormous range of "angry problems," nearly all people have some difficulty handling anger. The price paid for the distortion of a basic emotion is incalculable. Poor mental health, poor physical health, damage to relationships—especially to parent-child relationships—and even that most malignant of human diseases—*war*—are the wages of distorted anger.

Therefore it behooves us to understand and to work through our feelings about anger. As you read, you will see that insight into these feelings can free and make available many other feelings, talents, and potentials. A healthier *angry* outlook must lead to greater health, to improved parent-child relating, to a fuller life, and to success and happiness. Indeed, it can even be lifesaving.

T. I. R.

There is no rest for
a messenger 'til
the message is delivered.

Joseph Conrad—THE RESCUE

1

BEGINNINGS

In this section I want to describe some general considerations as well as some of the beginnings or origins of angry troubles.

Even the Saints

I assume the saints were human. I assume you are not a saint. All human beings get angry—and I'm sure the saints did, too. Feeling angry is a universal human phenomenon. It is as basic as feeling hungry, lonely, loving, or tired. The capacity to feel angry and to respond in some way to that feeling is in us from birth. Have you ever seen a newborn baby cry and scream and get red with rage? He does so usually in response to some increase in bodily tension or discomfort or frustration—the need for food or relief from the stick of a diaper pin, for example. Of course adults have their "tensions," and these are often born of very intricate, labyrinthlike dynamics. Sometimes the routes leading to feelings of anger are so convoluted and circuitous that it takes enormous skill to discern their original source, or fountainhead. *But* regardless of the reason for or the source of the anger or the relative ease or complexity in perceiving either the anger or its source—everybody, *but everybody*, gets angry. As you will see later on, this may not always be apparent. But it is so! The only exceptions are those poor unfortunate people who suffer from one or another form of severe brain damage.

Learning

Those of us who are physiologically whole are born with the potential to feel and to express anger. *But* the things that make us angry and the ways we feel and the things we do when we are angry are not the same for all of us. The particular, individual ways in which we respond are learned. Generally, no one sits down and gives us lessons. We learn in more effective ways—starting from the moment we are born.

Children are extremely perceptive and absorb what goes on around them long before they can talk or even comprehend language. They are like finely tuned receivers that pick up much more than is merely said. They are receptive and attuned to every mood, feeling, and change that goes on in people around them. They are particularly affected by the way their parents, sisters, and brothers feel and act. Many young children respond to a mother's "mood" long before she herself is consciously aware of its existence. This applies particularly to her approval and disapproval of how the child feels and acts.

Children do in fact "receive" and "record" what goes on around them, and they learn. They learn by doing over and over again—by repetition—and this doing is often initiated by imitation. They also learn by identification with a parent or relative. They learn by experimenting and testing, that is, by doing and then observing parental response to their actions. Of course all this applies to emotions and how the parents emote and respond to the child's feelings, especially the feeling—and expression—of anger.

Let Freedom Ring

Health is relative. There is no such thing as an absolute state of health or sickness. Everyone's physical, mental, and emotional condition is a combination of both. When health is preponderant, we are fortunate indeed—as we are when the emotional climate in which we were brought up, in which we live, and which we provide for our children promotes health.

A healthy emotional climate is first one in which all the emotions—especially anger—are given ample play and freedom. This is an atmosphere in which there is no dearth of emotional output or exchange. There is no emotional vacuum, nor does one kind of emotional display exist to the exclusion of others. In this atmosphere emotional output is appropriate and consistent. In this atmosphere it is *easy* to know what people feel. It is especially easy to know when they are angry. This is so because feelings—all kinds—are accepted and the conveying of how one feels is accepted openly and freely without threat of dire reprisal. In this environment no feeling or its expression is labeled "good" or "bad." This climate is not designed for the manufacture of saints or sinners. It is meant for human beings who have ordinary emotional responses and the need to express them freely. In this climate a child readily picks up the prevalence of consistency, openness, and warmth regarding all feelings. In effect, this atmosphere says to the child: "It is all right to feel love, and it is all right to feel anger. It is all right to express love, and it is all right to express anger. Your feelings are welcome here, and we would like to know what they are. You are loved and accepted and safe with all your feelings. You needn't stifle any of them to *please* us.

Victims of Victims

So many of us are afraid to feel, afraid to express feelings, and afraid to have other people *feel toward us*. This is especially true when the feeling is anger. There are many of us in whom much emotional crippling has taken place. We can allow only so-called acceptable feelings to come through and then only with great care, constriction, and trepidation. For many of us the potential amplitude of feelings—the vitality, depth, richness, and intensity—is poor. For many of us our emotional displays are either very shallow (or utterly flat) or inappropriate or both. Those of us who suffer in this way are almost certainly former (and present) inhabitants of "sick" emotional climates. Blaming parents or relatives will not help. We are the victims of victims, and we, too, shall produce victims unless we choose to change ourselves and the immediate emotional climate through understanding.

What about a sick emotional climate?

This is an environment in which people often feel one way but act another way. When they are angry, they smile sweetly or freeze and do nothing at all. In any case, there is a paucity of straight, honest, simply and readily definable expressions of feelings. In this environment, there is sometimes a serious dearth of strong feelings, often to the point of emotional vacuum. Usually what look like appropriate, strong emotional responses are actually superficial, hysterical, manipulative outbursts turned on and off like summer showers. These serve to confuse further and to subvert real feelings. This is an environment in which hysteria may suddenly give way to inhibition and even to paralysis of emotional expression. In this atmosphere small issues will evoke large displays and large issues will evoke nothing. This atmosphere will be marked by many intricate inconsistencies that the child can't possibly understand. This will be particularly so with anger and may result in an avoidance of anger and subsequent crippling in this very important emotional area. In effect, the victim will be told the following: "It is all right for me to get angry in this circumstance but not you." "Sometimes it is all right for you to get angry, but sometimes you can't, even though the circumstances are identical. It all depends on my mood—

which there is no way of knowing." "Why can't you be like me—I never get angry, but when I do, I don't show it. All I do is get cold and sullen and withdraw my attention and affection from you." "If you get angry, I'll know you don't love me." "Nice boys and girls don't get angry—especially at adults." "If you must get angry, at least be polite." "If you get angry, you will not be liked." "If you continue to get angry, you will surely get into great trouble." "Civilized people don't get angry, but if you get angry I'll have to tell Daddy, and he will get angry and will have to punish you when he gets home."

Parents in this environment will very often produce what is known as a double-bind situation which goes like this: "Don't hold it in—I can't stand when you do—let it out! But when you let it out, I will hit you for being disrespectful." This damned-if-you-do, damned-if-you-don't approach promotes severe conflict, much anxiety, great angry problems, and emotional paralysis.

Two Big Blocks

These are big destructive *blocks* to feeling and showing anger. Let's look at them, one at a time.

I call the first one "the secret pact" or "the be a nice guy—don't make waves" syndrome. The terms of the secret pact are very simple: *"I won't get angry, and therefore I will be sure that you don't get angry."* The pact is secret because the other party, especially if he's a person who feels free to get angry, doesn't know it exists. In any case, "don't-make-wavers" are generally people who predicate their whole lives and personalities on being "nice guys" and on being universally liked. Of course they feel that anger, especially if it shows, will destroy the image they live by. These people feel that any show of anger—even minor irritation—will alienate the other fellow. This is seen as an immediate threat to one's "nice guy" status and involves a potential loss of love. Since being universally loved is seen as the only way to be safe in this world, anger—especially anger that causes retaliation by the other fellow—is of course felt as a terrible threat. The "nice guy" is therefore forced into constantly playing a role. The price he pays for this role-playing is enormous. He can never be himself, and he expends enormous energy in attempting to fool himself and other people. Sadly none of this works. He seduces no one into liking him. Those that like him will like him in any case, and those that don't, won't. Even more sadly, blocking off anger ultimately destroys the very thing the "nice guy" wants—namely *love*. But more about this and other destructive effects later on. Suffice it here to say that the need to be universally liked, to ruffle no one's feelings, serves as an enormous block to the natural free feel and flow of anger.

The other big block, ultimately just as destructive, is the mind-your-own-business syndrome. The "emotional isolationist" honestly believes that if he doesn't get involved with other people, he won't get hurt. Of course anger, in any of its manifestations, is seen as a threat to his noninvolvement status. He must not get angry, let alone show it, because this would indicate *caring enough to get angry*. He sees this kind of caring as leading to involvement, emotional snares, and all kinds of *people traps*. He would rather "cool it and keep safe." Of course the ostrich phenomenon doesn't work.

Man is a community creature and cannot function in isolation. However ingeniously the emotional isolationist plots his course, emotional investment in other people and their investment in him will be inevitable. The only effect "cooling it" will have is to deprive him of the enormous benefits healthy, open social intercourse brings. "Cooling" anger will also contribute to the many poisons I will describe later on.

I want to close this chapter by saying that *blocking anger* makes us even greater "don't-make-wavers" and emotional isolationists, thus completing a very destructive vicious cycle.

One Smaller Block

The effects of this block are exactly the same in destructive value as those of the two big blocks. I call this one a smaller block only because people suffering from it have slightly less difficulty getting angry than those with the big blocks.

This "smaller block" is the need for control or mastery. People who have this need feel that angry feelings or a show of anger may be evidence of loss of control. Since they predicate their lives and well-being on total control of themselves, others, and the total environment, potential loss of control is invariably felt as a great threat. Unlike the previous two blocks (which operate mainly in people whom Horney calls self-effacing or compliant and detached or resigned—the "don't-make-wavers" and the noninvolvement specialists), this smaller block occurs mostly in *expansive* people

(Horney's term) and does allow some feel and show of anger. However, this is seldom a healthy, warm anger, which I will describe later on. Expansive anger is usually used in the service of sadistic manipulation or outright bullying in controlling people. It is often dished out under the guise of benevolence, but it always involves domineering despotism. It is also used in conjunction with vindictiveness, sometimes providing the sick energy necessary for vindictiveness to take place. This sick and synthetic anger is stunted and distorted because of the victim's inordinate need to be admired, if not worshiped (as differentiated from being liked). Since real undiluted anger may result in a diminishment of admiration and is seen as a loss of control of one's self and others, it is blocked and viewed with fear and trepidation.

Based on an individual's character structure, one of the three blocks will be used predominantly. However, use of all the blocks may be evident in the same person.

2

PERVERSIONS

This part of The Angry Book *describes the all-important ways in which we pervert the normal, natural free feel and flow of anger. These are the principal methods we use to contribute to the slush fund of perverted emotions.*

Perverted anger provides a reservoir of emotional slush that poisons one's system and leads to all kinds of emotional infections.

Recognition of these "perverting methods" can be very helpful in cutting down "twisting" or the production of "poisons," which I will discuss in the next section.

Putting It Down

There are two principal ways in which we "put down" angry feelings and potential angry responses in an attempt to get rid of them.

One is born of much practice and is triggered so quickly that the victim is completely unaware that he had a feeling of anger at all. This kind of putting-down is automatic and instantaneous. The victim is thoroughly and completely cheated of awareness of his feeling. Of course, he is also cheated of a choice of action or response. This kind of "automatic" putting-down of anger is the result of years of conditioning. It is designed to keep the victim absolutely free of any recognizable threat to his supposed non-angry status or image. Since this kind of putting-down works on a completely unconscious level, it is perhaps the most malignant perversion of all. Automatic putting-down is particularly insidious because the victim continues to see himself as a "nice, mind-your-own-business, don't-make-waves" type, while his slush fund grows and the pus and its poisons spread—without any awareness on his part. Of course he has symptoms of all kinds. However, his total success at cheating himself of awareness of anger prevents him from connecting symptoms with putting-down. Perhaps you know people who use automatic putting-down to a great extent. These are some of the typical statements they make: "Me, I just never get angry." "There's just nothing important enough to get angry about." "Yes, I can see that he's arrogant, vindictive, and a cheat and a liar, but it just has no effect on me." "Can't be bothered." "I couldn't care less."

The second kind of putting it down occurs with completely conscious awareness. Here the victim knows that he is angry and even feels like reacting or responding in an angry way. But like all slush-accumulating victims, he also feels that he has a vested interest in not feeling or showing anger—let alone not getting angry with anybody else. So, he works hard at not being angry or at least at being only minimally angry if he can't obliterate the feeling altogether. This conscious putting anger down does permit the victim at least some awareness of what he feels and who he is (our feelings tell us who we are). However, he, too, keeps awareness minimal and immediately strives, with full awareness here, to put the anger down and out. If he has enough will power, he may kid himself into believing that he has succeeded. But it never really works. He may put the anger down, but he cannot put it out, however extraordinary his will power may be. He, too, will inevitably contribute to the slush fund. Here are some of the typical statements the conscious down-putter makes: "So I'm angry—that doesn't mean I have to give in to it. I just control it and put it out of my mind." "I take a cold shower and forget about it." "I take a tranquilizer in the daytime and a sleeping pill at night, and it all disappears." "I just take a long walk and forget it" "So I'm a little peeved—I put it down with a couple of shots of Scotch and forget it." "Me aggravate myself? Never! I just laugh it off." "He gets other people angry, but I'm just not going to let him or anyone else even touch me."

Putting It Off

This mechanism works on the principle of thinking that if you delay anger long enough, maybe it will go away. Well, it doesn't! It goes into the slush fund.

The victim of putting it off delays feeling anger and responding to it, either unconsciously, consciously, or both. This is the person who generally puts off problems, conflicts, decisions, responsibility, and doing whatever has to be done. He feels that if it *doesn't go away*, at least there may come a time when it will be safer to feel, to express, and to do. Actually his slush fund builds up, produces various "poisons," becomes full to the point of explosion, and makes him feel less and less capable of handling his angry feelings. This contributes still further to his putting it off and thus builds a very vicious circle. Even if he should experience some delayed angry reaction, it is usually stilted and has a very poor quality—the majority of it already having been contributed to the slush fund and twisted into many assorted "poisons." As I said above, this perversion can go on with full awareness ("Oh, I'll think about it later" or "I'll decide what to say when we're all cooled off"), without awareness, or with partial awareness. For the most part, however, putting it off goes on as an automatic unconscious process. The individual does not know that he is putting it off. He does this so *quietly* and *quickly* that he often shuts off his anger before he has a chance to become aware of its existence. Sometimes—when it is "safe" and too late (for his health)—he allows some of his feelings to come through. Here are some of the typical statements the off-putter makes (I'm sure you've heard them): "Why didn't I think of that earlier?" "Why do I always think of the right thing to say when it's too late?" "I didn't feel angry when it happened, still don't—just have had this banging headache since then." "He always baits me, and I'm so dumb I don't know he's doing it till afterwards." "If he were here now, I'd really tell him what I think." "Can you imagine that guy? Thinking about it *now* really makes me angry.

Putting It On

Putting it on is the process of removing anger from the person, place, thing, or event that we are actually angry at and putting it on a "safer" or less threatening person, place, thing, or event. For example, anger may be transferred from a frightening boss and put on a frightened wife. Though a glimmer of awareness may be present, putting it on usually occurs with complete unconsciousness. An "on-putter" can suddenly get angry at someone for no apparent reason, or he may become angry at an imagined hurt or inappropriately angry at a minor hurt. He may accumulate or exaggerate old hurts and put them on someone innocent without any rationale whatsoever. Exaggerations and accumulations can sometimes be quite violent and can also become chronic, especially when the slush fund is overflowing and finally breaks through the walls that dam it up. Victims of these exaggerations or accumulations may transfer a lifelong rage at their mothers to their wives or husbands. Others may become terribly bitter and cynical and spend a lifetime splattering everyone and everything with a loosened fund of old slush. Still others turn their anger from its actual and appropriate direction to themselves and become full of self-hate and suffer serious depression. Some with extraordinary irrational belief splash the slush bank onto others to the point of delusion, fear, and paranoid ideas ("Others want to kill me"). Of course, there are different degrees of putting it on as well as different degrees of inappropriateness. At times the victim will direct his self-hate to other people. At other times he will swear that other people hate him, here again projecting his self-hate. If the degree of self-hate and distortion is great enough, he may suffer from paranoid delusions—feeling that other people want to hurt or kill him. Most cases are not this severe but are still very destructive.

In any case, the main intent, conscious or unconscious, is to shift anger to the least threatening person, thing, event, or situation. (Thus a man dissatisfied with his job may chronically find fault with the way his wife keeps their home.) This is an attempt to maintain his working ability. Of course failure always stalks

on-putters. The on-putter in fact is one of the most fla-
grant destroyers of human relationships. He is dishon-
estly and inappropriately "nice" at the wrong times,
and he is consistently and inappropriately angry nearly
all the rest of the time—inevitably putting a great
strain on all his relationships, often to the point of
utter destruction.

Diluting It

With this mechanism the anger is felt but is immediately diluted in an attempt to render it impotent. Every kind of conceivable intellectual rationalization is used in this attempt. Anyone with the least bit of objectivity can see through the rationalization or dilution. The diluter, however, is anything but objective. He is highly subjective and has a vested interest in proving to himself and others that he is not angry. On a conscious level his dilutions may seem to work. However, his unconscious slush bank will grow as a result of his dilutions. Of course, he will not be aware of this growth, let alone its poisonous effects.

Here are some examples of common dilutions:

"He must be sick. I know that he can't help it. So I can't possibly get angry at him."

"Rational, logical, civilized people keep cool heads.

They are controlled by their heads. They don't get angry. Only fools get angry."

"Oh, I know she'll be sorry about it tomorrow, so how can I be angry with her?"

"One doesn't get angry at children!"

"What gives you the idea that I'm irritated? I haven't even raised my voice."

"I just do something else and the feeling goes away."

"No so loud, please—other people will hear you. So vulgar, you know."

"It only looks like anger—it's not really so."

"So who is angry?"

"I'm not shouting and I'm not angry. I am speaking more intensely than usual only because I'm vitally interested in the topic we are discussing."

Let me give an example of one last, particularly insidious, dilution—which of course takes many forms (some of the above are variations of it, to some extent): "I understand his distress, and I simply turn the other cheek—and forgive him." This is used in an attempt to dilute anger and at the same time to add to one's all-forgiving "nice guy" status. Of course the more the individual manages to convince himself of his "nice guy" role, the more crippled he will be in the all-important angry department of his emotions. Thus he manages to use dilution to build a subtle but destructive vicious circle.

Freezing It

Freezing it is the total perversion. It combines the perversions I've already described with its own peculiar refinements. We can say that if there was an accurate way (and there isn't) to measure the degree of perverting anger, we would then know the degree of freezing it The various perversions are not mutually exclusive. We—all of us—combine putting it off, and putting it down, and so on. Some of us use one perversion more than another. Those of us with great angry problems will undoubtedly make much use of all the perversions. Our healthier confreres will pervert anger to a lesser degree. The particular combination of perversions (or the particular perversion we use most) will depend on our total personal histories and character structures. Of course, *consciousness* and *unconsciousness* regarding our difficulties with anger and our perverting of anger will also be relative and will exist in varied combinations. In any case, the destructive effect will be directly proportional to the degree of perverting. Perverting, whatever the degree, will however always be destructive. It will result in a slush fund of perverted anger, providing ample material for conversion to assorted poisons discussed in Part 3. If it were possible, a measure of the reservoir of slush, of the assorted poisons, of the degree of perverting, or of a combination of all would indicate the degree of freezing it.

Freezing it is the measure of success in subverting anger. It never works on anger exclusively. It always affects all our emotions, including love. It is a measure of our total success in removing ourselves from our feelings (especially anger). In removing ourselves from our feelings—that is, in submerging and deadening our feelings—we are extraordinarily destructive of ourselves. This is a form of self-imposed anesthesia (like ether or gas) that kills our spontaneity, sensitivity, and potential creativity. It is the great destroyer of *self* and *human identity* and *human relatedness.* How can we relate if we don't feel? We cannot feel with a frozen finger, and we cannot feel with frozen emotions. As with a frozen limb, an emotional gangrene sets in which, in feeling tone, removes us from humanity—from ourselves and other people. Freezing it—removing one's self from what one feels by whatever means and measures, that is, perverting and deadening one's feelings—may well be considered the total measure of emotional pathology or neurosis in a human being.

3

TWISTING IT: THE ASSORTED POISONS

Unfortunately, the twisting I refer to here has nothing to do with anything as gay and alive as dancing.

Perversion has resulted in a conversion of healthy angry feelings and responses into a slush bank. This fund of perverted anger or slush does not just sit there inert. It, too, somehow, must be expressed, however crippled that final expression may be. "Twisting" refers to the process of creating these distorted expressions— which may happen sooner or later or sooner and later but does in fact always happen. The slush accumulated from perverting anger will eventually be twisted into grotesque shapes, here called "poisons." These poisons may be so distorted or so subtle that they will not be recognizable as anger at all. At times it will be almost impossible to see any relationship between a poison and simple healthy feelings and expressions of anger. These poisons are further distorted by other sick personality aspects and in turn makes the individual even sicker emotionally, thus creating all kinds of complicated emotional vicious circles. Twisting or converting emotional slush to poison is for the most part an unconscious process. The individual does this automatically, without awareness. Likewise, he almost never associates a particular poison with anger. There is nothing clear-cut or well delineated here. Some of the poisons seem very much alike. This is so especially because there is much overlapping and intertwining. The poisons are not mutually exclusive; that is, one person can and usually does make use of many of the poisons at the same time. There are subtle differences between them though, and it is important to understand them if we are to understand the total effect. Of course the effect—as with every malignancy—is always the same. Perverted anger twisted into grotesque forms must eventually poison one's self as well as one's relationships with others. This of course contributes enormously to anxiety, as well as to other neurotic manifestations and concomitant misery. It is therefore important that we recognize the various forms of poison as part of an effort to reverse sick processes in active pursuit of change, growth, and better health.

Anxiety

A great deal of emotional slush is constantly being twisted into anxiety. Anxiety is derived from many sources—emotional conflicts, hurt pride, loss of self-esteem, and so on, *but* much of it is derived directly from the slush bank. Indeed, it is my belief that the slush bank provides the principal fuel of anxiety-producing machinery.

Anxiety itself is a highly complicated subject on which many papers and books have been written. It is not our purpose to write another one here. However, anxiety as the almost inseparable and sometimes indistinguishable blood brother of perverted anger (slush) is certainly a major poison and therefore deserving of our attention.

Slush can be twisted into anxiety that is then felt as *primitive anxiety in its raw form.* Or slush can be twisted into anxiety that then produces all kinds of complicated symptoms. These symptoms are then a response to slush and anxiety. These symptoms are designed to dissipate and to combat the very slush and anxiety that produced the symptoms in the first place. An "anxiety attack" derived from twisting slush often occurs in an individual fearful of anger, who feels possible loss of control in an impending emergence of anger.

Anxiety in its raw, or primitive, form may be felt both emotionally and physically (the anxiety attack). The victim may feel fearful mildly or to the point of panic, with a feeling of dissolution, "of coming apart," of loss of self or identity, of a sense of doom without being able to tell why. The feeling may be accompanied by heart palpitations, flushing, shaking, chills, sweats, gastrointestinal upsets, severe headache, nausea, neck stiffening, muscle cramps, and so on. These symptoms may exist alone or in any combination and in any degree of intensity. Anxiety in a complicated form can result in any number of emotional disorders, either acute and relatively short-lived or chronic and of life-long duration. These may include disorders of personality or character resulting in stilted, rigid, codified kinds of behavior—invariably destructive to one's self, one's relationships, and one's functioning in all areas. Anxiety can also result in any number of recognizable symptoms of emotional disorder. These include depressions, obsessions (fixed irrational preoccupations or ideas or irrational beliefs), irrational compulsions (the need to do certain things again and again even though there is no obvious rationale for the action), phobias (inordinate, irrational fears—of bridges, closed places, trains, heights, and so on), severe insomnia, etc. As I said before, these symptoms are a way of mitigating anxiety. Unfortunately, they are themselves highly destructive and also produce additional anxiety and symptoms, again activating very vicious circles.

Indeed, it has been said that anxiety is the fuel that keeps the motor of neurosis running. For our purposes, however, it is important to remember that perverted anger is a major force producing and sustaining anxiety. All the poisons that follow will stem from perversion of the slush bank. But many will also have their roots in anxiety. If we consider perverted anger as mother of the poisons (anxiety included as a major poison and therefore as a child), then perhaps we may consider anxiety as an incestuous father.

Depression

Where there is anxiety there is bound to be depression and vice versa. I have never seen clinical evidence of depression without signs of concomitant raw anxiety. Depression may be mild or severe, acute or chronic, periodic (in regular on-and-off phases) or sporadic. It has a cause, but the cause may be elusive and impossible to discern. Depression is always painful and destructive, sometimes to the point of paralysis. It may completely destroy one's ability to function and rob one of every semblance of happiness. Depression, however, is not always severe and incapacitating. It can also be subtle and chronic—so chronic, in fact, that its victim may have no awareness that he is depressed. I have seen patients who have been depressed for so many years that they forgot what it is like to feel otherwise. Only at their first sign of getting well did they awake to the fact that they had been "somber and heavy-hearted" for years.

While there may be very natural reasons for depression (though often the reasons are quite neurotic), it cannot continue without benefit of a slush fund. One may be depressed because of loss of a loved one, but continued depression needs a slush fund to fuel it. Depression almost always derives from twisting. This poison is produced by turning anger inward upon oneself. Sustained depression equals sustained self-hate. Some victims know they hate themselves. They spend hours haranguing themselves—torturing themselves and telling all who will listen how dastardly they are. Other victims have no idea they are self-hating. But they are sometimes depressed enough to commit suicide. It is appropriate to be sad at a loss, but to hate oneself, to sustain hatred of oneself for that loss, is invariably self-punishing, neurotic, perverse, poisonous, and destructive.

Guilt, Overeating, Self-Imposed Starvation

These seem like strange bedfellows, but they are really close relatives. They almost never exist without depression. Sometimes the depression is obvious; often it is nowhere to be seen, safely tucked away. But you can bet it is there, just below the surface. You have only to consider the self-destructive processes involved to appreciate the necessary twisting into self-hate. Depression must be there, and sometimes it emerges in clear clinical form as soon as the overeating or starvation stops.

I myself in practice have yet to see these symptoms in other than extremely angry people. Unfortunately, these people did not express anger normally. Many of them hardly felt angry at all, but they all had huge slush funds—and they busily and unconsciously twisted slush into these poisons. This was true of the perpetually jolly fat girl who without her awareness ate even more than her usual huge quantities each time her anger was provoked. "Normal" people would have become angry. She ate but took months to connect (deeply and feelingwise) her anger and its repression with eating. She eventually lost weight but only with much work and insight. This was also true of the skinny, appetiteless, dour man and the woman who perpetually felt guilty for an interminable list of supposed crimes she couldn't possibly have been connected with. Of course the guilt as well as the overeating and starvation were all means these people used for turning anger on themselves, attempting to dissipate it but hating themselves and punishing themselves even more. Think of the self-hate involved in starving oneself, in torturing oneself with a chronic burden of guilt, with stuffing oneself with food to the point of bodily distortion, nausea, and self-revulsion. Think of the poisonous effects on one's self as well as on one's relationships with other people—again having repercussions upon oneself. The poisonous possibilities are infinite. Believe it or not, it sometimes happens that "fat people" (obsessive eaters), guilt-ridden people, and "skinny people" (completely unable to eat, sometimes requiring force feeding or intravenous infusions) trade or switch symptoms, doing complete turnabouts. I knew two grossly obese women who not only lost weight but eventually starved themselves to a severe underweight state of malnutrition. It took much treatment before they regained a semblance of "normal appetite." This is not really surprising when we realize that although upbringing and environment may be different in these people, the underlying causes of symptoms are often similar and even identical.

No Sleep and Sleep Sleep

No sleep and sleep sleep are two more poisonous, depressed bedfellows.

Twisting slush can lead to enormous restlessness, anxiety, a compulsive onslaught of multitudinous thoughts—all impossible conditions for sleeping. Insomnia is very commonly concomitant with depression. It is very difficult to sleep when one is seething with perverted anger. The victim is often completely unaware of the anger but complains desperately of agitation that prevents sleep.

Some depressed people sleep a great deal of the time. Sleep sleep is largely an attempt to escape the pain of their self-flagellation. I have known chronically depressed patients—unaware that they were attempting to escape life (a heavyhearted, depressed kind of life, as it were)—who literally slept two-thirds of the time. Such sleep serves as a self-imposed general anesthesia.

When people suffering from insomnia or over-sleeping are finally put in touch with their anger, the beneficial results can be very dramatic and gratifying to behold. It sometimes takes considerable time for them to know that they are angry, to accept their anger, and to express it and live it through with feeling. But when they do, the relief that follows is dramatic indeed. I remember a woman I saw in treatment who spent at least ten years sleeping about two hours a night. This in itself had a terribly debilitating and depressing effect. She said that the worst part of her not sleeping was that terrible thoughts popped into her head as she lay in bed. For a long time she refused to describe these thoughts and could not even entertain the idea that feelings associated with these thoughts were keeping her awake. After we had established a close and trusting relationship and she was certain that I would not "judge her harshly," she revealed the thoughts of her sleepless nights. They involved visual fantasies of terrible things happening to her mother and sister. As treatment progressed, she realized that she had a severe problem with anger and especially anger toward loved ones. After a while she became aware of ancient (stemming from earliest childhood) angry feelings toward her mother and sister. As she was able to feel, accept, and express (with a good deal of emotion) these feelings, the thoughts vanished and sleep ensued. This was no simple matter. For this to happen, her attitude toward anger plus her unrealistic angelic image of herself had to be changed, which required much self-examination in all areas and realistic self-acceptance. We both worked hard and the results were very gratifying.

Tomorrow and Tomorrow: Chronic Anticipation, Obsessive Ruminating, Peculiar Thoughts

These poisons are still a few other depressed bedfellows. Much slush is twisted into useless anticipation of events that have no importance or will never occur or over which there can be no control. Much slush is twisted into obsessive ruminating or endless, useless, intertwined worries that go on with no object other than self-torture, self-deception (avoidance of anger), and dissipation of perverted anger. There are people who spend half a lifetime and nearly all their energy in self-destructive preoccupation with pasts that cannot be undone and futures that will never arrive. These first two bedfellows—chronic anticipation and obsessive ruminating—are particularly evident in very angry, depressed people who have particularly large slush funds. Of course they have no idea that they are angry. How many times I've heard these statements linked together: "If only I could stop this damn thinking. I just worry, worry, worry a million thoughts. I feel I'm going to bust, as if I'm coming apart at the seams." Of course what they are coming apart with is buried rage—but they don't know that.

What about peculiar thoughts? I discussed them at some length in *The Winner's Notebook*, but they certainly deserve some discussion here in this special reference. Slush is frequently converted to "peculiar thoughts," often with no obvious connection whatsoever. These thoughts include illogical sentences that defy understanding; irrational and seemingly untimely thoughts; and odd, sometimes grotesque and frightening, fantasies. They occur most often at times when one's guard is down—such as just before going to sleep, periods of great fatigue, periods of great anxiety, sudden responses of anger to unexpected or subtle stimulation. Generally, new anger and old slush will be perverted and twisted into the most grotesque forms when great attempts are made to deny them. A little perverted anger held back again and again often snowballs enormously and emerges in some very peculiar and frightening ways. Let me give you a few examples from my own clinical experience.

One of my patients at certain times "saw himself" running through a subway train screaming berserkly. It turned out that this fantasy occurred each time he looked for a job. He apparently saw his looking for a job as demeaning and hated himself for needing to take the subway in order to look. This rage at himself was expressed in the self-ridiculing fantasy of running through the train berserk.

Another patient had "terrible thoughts" concerning her mother. She used to think of her mother as lost, starving, dying of a malignant disease, being crushed by falling buildings, and so on. For a long time she denied feeling angry at her mother. When the full extent of her anger was felt, accepted, and expressed, her "bad thoughts" disappeared.

Another woman I saw in treatment had "bad thoughts" regarding her infant son. Most of them involved her fear of killing him. When she realized and worked through her anger at him (largely for burdening her with an unwanted responsibility), she was relieved of the thoughts.

Peculiar thoughts are not a sign of madness. People almost always know that they are "peculiar," thus demonstrating considerable sanity. People almost never act out a thought. These thoughts are, however, very often evidence of angry problems. Sometimes if the thoughts are very disturbing and frequent, professional help is needed to work out the angry problems involved.

Traps: Obsessions, Compulsions, Phobias

These are complicated emotional syndromes or sets of symptoms. They are always linked to anxiety. They may be considered as emotional traps that are almost impossible to escape without professional help. Sometimes they are linked to perverted anger, as is often the case with anxiety itself. Irrational sets of ideas, beliefs, and preoccupations may consist of one or more sets of "peculiar thoughts"—for example, my patient's obsessive thoughts about hurting her little son. Compulsions—or the inordinate, uncontrollable need to do something over and over again without apparent rationale—as well as phobias (irrational fears) often have many roots, but I have often found very long roots connecting down to perverted anger.

I remember a patient of mine who was terribly afraid (without apparent reason) of red trucks. This fear would be so great at times that he couldn't leave his house. The sound of a fire truck was enough to terrify him. When he went places with his wife, she sometimes guided him—while he kept his eyes closed. She often became embarrassed because people, thinking he was blind, looked at them with obvious pity. Much psychoanalytic work, including a great deal of probing and investigating, revealed many personality and emotional problems. These were not easily soluble. This patient required many hours of hard work, establishing insights and linkages regarding past and present memories, attitudes, and feelings, before he was relieved of what was becoming an increasingly paralyzing and painful symptom. Like most psychiatric symptoms this one was multifaceted, but one large facet or root involved an extreme fear of angry impulses stemming from a very sick outlook regarding anger. What finally came out was that red equaled anger and that trucks represented instruments of aggression. Red trucks put this man in touch with his own angry feelings and impulses (of course, he had a huge, potentially explosive, slush fund) of which he was terrified.

Not all fears are as well defined, developed, and destructive as the above. Many of us who have difficulties with anger are only vaguely aware of "uneasy feelings" at "different times" or with "certain people" or in "certain circumstances." Not all of us need professional help. But with improved "angry insight" we can all gain and grow and become easier, freer, and happier people.

"No, No, No! A Thousand Times No!"—Denial

One of the ways people cope with unpleasant confrontations is to avoid them. Sometimes when they can't avoid them, they simply deny their existence. This is also true of unwanted feelings and conflicts. Of course, this applies to anger and especially anger that will result in difficult conflict. Sometimes blatant confrontations with obvious truth makes denial very difficult. Denial is sometimes made possible by a variety of complicated psychological devices. Some of these psychological devices have a peculiar way of going in and out of style. When one considers that a particular time and a particular place produce cultural pressures characteristic of the time and place in question, one sees that this is not so peculiar after all.

For example, in Victorian times ladies were not

supposed to have "indecent" sexual feelings. But they had them, and they denied having them. When sexual impulses and fantasies made ordinary denial impossible, they diverted these feelings to physiological areas that served as outlets as well as a form of anesthesia or denial. Thus some Victorian ladies suffered from paralysis of both legs for no physiological reason whatsoever. It was as if a self-imposed, unconscious hypnosis took place that saved them from sexual feelings or conflict. How could a lady who is paralyzed from the waist down have sexual feelings or worries? We don't see many of these "conversion hysterias" anymore. But people still occasionally develop conversion symptoms to avoid confrontation with anger. Of course they also develop all kinds of other symptoms, too, some of which we have already spoken about, such as anxiety and depression.

I remember one woman with a paralysis of the right arm who constantly dreamed of stabbing her husband—with her right arm. She was completely unaware of feeling any anger toward him. She likewise denied any recognition of meaning in her dream even though the meaning was quite obvious. As a matter of fact, only months after treatment started did she remember having this repetitive dream. But not all escapes or denials of angry feelings are this obvious. I had a patient in treatment who was 150 pounds overweight. She saw herself as a sweet, good-natured, jovial, angelic kind of person who never got angry. But she did realize that there were angry times when she went on huge eating binges that actually lasted through several days and nights. It finally became clear that these binges occurred whenever she became enraged. They were really the equivalent of temper tantrums, but very self-destructive ones, to say the least. They were her way of avoiding and denying anger. Despite her self-imposed picture of herself as angelic, this woman was capable of great rage. Obviously she preferred to be fat and "sweet" rather than angry, thin, and healthy. After much work and many new insights, she accepted her anger—and worked much of it off along with her fat.

Denial is a form of twisting since it deals with old perverted anger. But it can also be considered a perversion since it is used to pervert current angry feelings.

Self-Sabotage

In her various works, Karen Horney has brilliantly described the complicated role of self-hate. Its most important function is to keep its victim striving for impossible and "ideal" goals in quest of neurotic glory. Each failure to be gloriously ideal is met with self-hate, which in effect provides the whip to push the victim up the impossible trail again and again. In any case, the slush fund provides ample fuel to turn on oneself in the service of self-hate. Poisonous vehicles in the service of self-hate come in an almost endless variety of forms. Indeed, nearly all the poisons contain some element of self-hate. At this point, however, I want to mention a few miscellaneous poisons I've run into in practice which were obviously self-destructive. I say obviously only because it was obvious to me. More often than not, the patient had no idea that he was engaged in twisting and in self-hating enterprises.

A very blatant form of self-hate is *accident prone-ness*. Its victims are somehow involved in accident after accident with no awareness of their purposeful involvement. I saw one woman who sustained four fractures in three auto accidents as well as multiple minor injuries, including several kitchen-knife lacerations that required suturing.

One woman I saw had had six unwanted pregnancies before she became aware of the anger toward herself that was involved each time.

Another woman lost an object she valued highly each time she felt that she failed at being the "ideal wife and mother" (incidentally, a battalion of people working in perfect harmony could not possibly have fulfilled her concept of "ideal"). For a long time she blamed her losing of things on simple "carelessness."

I have also seen any number of accident- and sickness-prone persons unconsciously motivated by slush turned in on themselves. One woman, not content to suffer several fractures and automobile accidents, ran from doctor to doctor until she finally managed to have her gall bladder, appendix, and uterus removed. She had no idea that these were in any way onslaughts on herself.

A man I knew would wait until he was firmly entrenched in a superb job and doing beautifully, then would manage to make mistake after mistake. If he wasn't fired, he'd arrive at work later and later. On one job he actually stayed away days at a time until he was finally fired. He said there was "something that kept me away," but he couldn't explain what.

I remember a man who had had rheumatic fever who knew that upper respiratory infections could be fatal but who always managed to get sore throats. I say and mean *managed* because without fail this man made it a point (without awareness) to get chilled, wet in cold, rainy weather, and overtired when it would have been much easier to take proper care of himself.

Of course there are also many subtle manifestations of self-sabotage, though I must say that familiarity with them makes them seem anything but subtle. I think of patients I've had with an uncanny knack for forming disastrous relationships including extraordinarily masochistic ones. One woman I saw in consultation had managed to marry three alcoholic men, each of whom nearly beat her to death. I think of the people I've known who insist on continuing in self-destructive, completely unprofitable relationships. We all know people who always manage to take jobs well below their ability or potential. We also know people who do well for a while and then somehow but inevitably manage to lose all the profits of their efforts on a "good deal" that turns out to be a disaster. Have you known any severe alcoholics, drug addicts, or chronic gamblers? Obsessive gambling and alcoholism are complicated illnesses, but think of the self-hate involved that literally drags a man into the gutter. I have interviewed gamblers who feel relieved of tension only after they have lost everything and are absolutely ruined. The list obviously goes on and on. Self-sabotage can be acute or chronic, subtle or blatant, mild or severe enough to result in loss of life (there are people who insist on working in disaster areas or as daredevils). Self-sabotage often has many roots and can be extraordinarily complicated. *But* I have yet to see a case that was not fed by perverted anger, and I have seen cases in which self-hate was the prime motivating force.

Sweet, Sweet, Sweet, and the Blood Pressure Goes Up, Up, Up

"He got so angry he nearly had apoplexy." This wouldn't be likely if he expressed his anger. It is the man who gets angry and manages to hide it completely whose blood pressure goes up enough so that he has a stroke. There is no question that slush poisons us physically. I'm sure that it contributes to attacks on the digestive system, circulatory system, respiratory system—indeed, on all the systems. Chronically sitting there, it undoubtedly adds its share to whatever faulty physiology already exists, not to mention any disease or bodily dyscrasia that may develop later. It is impossible to evaluate its exact role, that is, to measure its influence exactly. But can you picture a man bottled up with angry slush functioning well physiologically? It is likewise impossible to measure accurately the role of perverted anger in psychosomatic disturbances. But physicians and psychiatrists with ample clinical experience will hardly deny its enormous role. Let us talk a bit here about psychosomatic illness. It will help us to shed some light on perverted anger and its deleterious physiological effects on the poisons we call "psychosomatic illnesses."

First, it is important to realize that thoughts, feelings, sick feelings, and regular physical functions all take place in one body. In that body nothing can take place without having an effect on everything else. The ears receive sound waves and the eyes receive light waves that convey messages to the brain, in which is integrated information that perhaps makes us angry. This feeling is felt by the entire body: messages are sent out by chemical changes in nerves so that various hormones are excreted, heart rate changes, the diameter of blood vessels change, and so on. These effects in turn affect the skin, musculature, digestive tract, lungs—all the systems and organs of the body. Messages that are smooth and free-flowing will have concomitant healthy physical expression and counterparts. Messages that are polluted will have poisonous physical repercussions.

Some people confuse psychosomatic illness with hypochondria. They are not at all the same. With hypochondria (which also often has self-hating poison elements), the illness is imagined. A psychosomatic illness is real indeed. The cause of origin of the illness is emotional, *but* the sickness is a demonstrable lesion. There is a malfunction that can be demonstrated or seen by some clinical means—auscultation (stethoscope), palpitation (feeling with fingers and hands), percussion (finger tapping), x-ray, laboratory diagnoses, and so on. Gastric duodenal ulcer may have psychological roots, but the erosion in the stomach or duodenum is a physical entity. The same is true of certain skin lesions, the afflicted bronchi of asthmatic patients, and so forth.

As with all other human sicknesses, dysplasias, or malfunctions, psychosomatic illnesses always have multiple, complicated roots. But again—here as elsewhere—the slush fund contributes a major share of evil energy. I have seen a number of asthmatics who were enormously relieved and who could finally breathe when they learned how to weep. Strange but true that so many of us have somehow lost the ability for normal weeping. Closer investigation however revealed that some of these weepers were not crying in pain or misery or pity or self-pity. They were actually crying with rage, and it wasn't weeping ability that was perverted so much as their angry feelings and expression.

I remember a man who was brought up as a Quaker and whose image of himself was one of complete lack of anger. If he had really lacked anger, this would have been fine. But though he managed always to be sweet, sweet, sweet, and he did in fact fool himself, his family, and his friends, he could not fool his arteries and his blood pressure. After an initial small stroke, psychoanalysis revealed an enormous slush fund of an explosive proportion, which, in fact, was beginning to explode via arteries in his brain. He was only forty years old, but the taut bow he carried within himself was drawn tight beyond endurance. Of course all internists, surgeons, and psychiatrists have seen their share of sweet, sweet, sweet people who suffered from peptic ulcer, colitis, and ileitis sometimes to the point of perforation, hemorrhage, and death.

Apparently, it is easier to fool oneself than one's digestive tract. Migraine headache is another malady commonly seen in psychiatric practice. I have had patients who have visited any number of neurologists, neurosurgeons, and headache clinics to no avail. For a long while many of them refused psychiatric referral, feeling that there was nothing "crazy" about them. They were right. One does not have to be "crazy" to handle anger in a crazy way. I have many times seen a good strong temper tantrum bring immediate temporary relief. Prolonged relief invariably involves prolonged treatment, re-evaluation, and re-orientation regarding attitudes and actions vis-à-vis anger.

I would like to note here that the muscles are particularly affected by slush. This is not hard to understand when we think of how we tense ourselves in response to various emotions. Some of the worst cases of chronic stiff neck are due to perverted anger. Extreme muscular stiffness is seen in catatonia, which is discussed in the next chapter.

The skin is a particularly good showplace of how we feel, which seems natural enough when we consider that it derives from the same sensitive embryonic tissue as the brain and nervous system. Have you thought about how one's skin responds to embarrassment (blushing), anger (redness), fear (sweating), terror (hair standing up and goose flesh), as well as how the skin appears in general states of health and well-being and in sickness? It is also unfortunately a vehicle for the expression of slush. I do not say this is true of every skin disease, but there are many that would be aided considerably by a better angry outlook. I remember a woman I had in treatment who suffered from a very severe, ugly lesion that covered most of her body. Grossly, it appeared raw, grated, and weepy and in many places did not look like skin at all. She had been to many doctors to no avail. Salves, solutions, sun rays, and so on, did not help her. As a matter of fact, she became progressively worse. She finally consented to see a psychiatrist, but she did not want any kind of psychoanalytic treatment. She was given tranquilizers and energizers but only got worse. She was then given a series of electric shock treatments, which helped relieve some of the depression she had developed by then but which had no effect on her skin one way or another. Eventually she came to see me. Marcy was an extremely self-effacing, compliant woman who spent most of her early treatment hours in an effort to convince me of how really happy she was, except for her skin. She said that her childhood was a very happy one, without incident, and that she couldn't remember ever having had a fight with her sisters. She told me that she adored her dead father as well as her gentle, sweet, devoted mother (still alive). Her image of herself was very much like her image of her mother. She did not remember ever having been angry. The reason for her refusal to see a psychoanalyst soon became apparent. She simply did not wish to disturb a just-too-perfect image. And disturbed it became! After months of work—particularly of analysis of dreams—it became apparent that she did in fact love her father but was also happy that he had died.

These seemingly mutually exclusive emotional entities are extremely common in human psychology. Marcy felt that her father's death was revenge and a vindictive triumph over her mother. As time went on, the twisting of this rage to and through her skin became unnecessary. Strengthened by our relationship, she became aware that her anger did not kill her father nor did anger make her an evil person. For two years she did little else than report to me three times a week and sound off enormous anger—and as she did so, her skin cleared. Eventually the lesion disappeared and was replaced by healthy tissue. Much subsequent work relieved her of the need to be sweet and angelic (with an enraged skin). She chose instead just to be human.

It is very difficult to evaluate effects of the slush fund on human ills. Does it make us susceptible to viral infections? Does it increase our susceptibility to malignant disease? How much effect does it have on the heart, especially in people who already suffer from heart disease? I don't know. But it would not surprise me if its role is considerable. Poison will out, and when one's physiology is malfunctioning, it will undoubtedly be even more vulnerable than usual.

Talk, Talk, Talk, and No Talk

Anger—perverted anger—slush is sometimes converted to poisonous talk. This often takes the form of a great deal of seemingly nonsensical verbiage. It functions as a way to dissipate poisonous energy and is not unrelated to the mouth movement that takes place in compulsive overeating. However, if you listen very carefully to some very angry compulsive talkers (unconscious of their anger and not about to let anyone else directly in on it either), you may pick up some extraordinary hostile remarks, some of them subtle and some quite blatant. If confronted with the hostile intent of the remark, these talkers will either deny having made the remark or call you paranoid for your ridiculous interpretation. Some of these persons are what I call "sneak speakers." They dilute their hostile assaults with so much inappropriate verbal garbage that one hardly feels the knife as it slips between the ribs. I remember one woman who talked and talked and talked about all manner of things. In the middle of each verbal barrage, however, she always stealthily managed to twist the talk to the subject of husbands' deaths, widowhood, and insurance. She simply could not understand why her husband got irritated—even though he was still very much alive.

Another kind of sneak speaker who may be relatively quiet most of the time is the individual who always manages to find the one flaw in a plan, painting, party, situation, ambition, and so on. He does this as a sneak expression of poison, but when confronted with his wet-blanket effect, he will invariably tell you that he speaks as he does only for the sake of constructive truth. He will never admit his angry intent. How can he when he has a neurotic interest in not ever being angry, let alone sadistic? I call these sneaks the "but people." Here are some of their typical statements:

"That dress is nice, *but* it would be nicer if you lost weight."

"I love your apartment, *but* isn't it a little dark?"

"That's a great idea you have, *but* do you think you are really up to it?"

Of course they feel that others' anger at them is completely unjustified since "I'm only being honest." People are actually angry at them because they are being dishonest. Under the guise of truth, the sneak speakers are subtly but consistently barbing, snipping, and digging away. They never warmly, honestly, and in a straightforward way express what they really feel.

Then there is the reverse poison—mutism, relative or complete. There are people who will contain their anger and slush at any price, and the price is often catastrophic. Here, too, there are many variations, degrees, and intensities. There are people who say less and less as slush surfaces. The poison here is an attrition of words and expression. Some of these people can go without talking for weeks and even months. The effect on those close to them, particularly their mates, can be exquisitely cruel. It is like living with the walking dead. Sometimes a mate will scream, "Hit me, yell, scream, break something—do anything, but do something—talk, talk, talk!" but often to no avail. Of course the no-talker will deny any attempt at sadism or punishment in his mutism. He will deny that it can possibly be a form of poisonous vengeance. In effect, what many no-talkers are saying with their mutism is a facsimile of the following:

"I will punish you by depriving you of my feelings and words. I am cutting you off and out. You can bust, but you will not reach me." If you confront them with their cruelty, they will say that you are crazy: "I wasn't even angry—just didn't feel like talking."

Mutism can be carried to a particularly malignant and destructive degree. One form of severe emotional disturbance is a catatonic schizophrenic reaction. With this sickness an individual completely cuts himself off from the world, remaining inert, stiff (physically rigid), and mute for days, weeks, months, and even years. Forced feeding and intravenous feeding often must be implemented to keep him alive. For all intents and purposes, he seems like a complete vegetable. Yet this is an emotional illness that many specialists believe is intimately related to enormous rage and total inability to express it. It is almost as if the individual's total organism is dedicated to a complete stance against any expression whatsoever in order to make sure that no affect or emotion leaks through.

Though the dynamics and other features of the illnesses are different, the similarity in catatonic reactions and very severe depressions is striking. This applies to outward appearance as well as to the great angry difficulties involved in both.

In general, schizophrenic patients—noncatatonic, too—demonstrate a very flattened or shallow kind of emotional response. Many talk in a monotone devoid and obviously divested of feeling. This is often an attempt to divorce the world and themselves completely from what they feel—especially strong angry feelings. Interestingly, people who get over these reactions, including catatonic ones, indicate that they are in fact very much in touch with the world around them. Remarkably, some remember every word that was said to and around them during their catatonic state, even though they never responded. For some, the reaction is described as almost a giant temper tantrum—a great hurt-pride reaction that did not permit them to utter a word. Many patients later report some very hostile wish-fulfilling fantasies, even though they were not in touch with their anger. Some picture great torture and execution scenes and all kinds of bizarre deaths involving great numbers of people. Some picture destruction of the world. Fantasies of this kind are well known to occur among highly disturbed people and are commonly called (psychiatric parlance) "world destruction fantasies." Indeed, for these people the world is destroyed since they have cut themselves and their feelings off from the rest of the world. These fantasies are excellent evidence of great slush funds, but too often their victims are too sick to connect them with feelings of any anger at all.

Interestingly, these people sometimes sustain a condition called "catonic excitement" in which they undergo a complete transformation. They flail about, sometimes inflicting great damage on themselves and anyone else within reach. It is as if all that was previously held in check has finally broken loose.

Let's Pretend:
Imitations of Anger

There are two main imitations of anger. They are both poisons and are particularly insidious because they look like the real thing. They are at best synthetic products and stunted forms that do not bring real relief to their users. They further serve to confuse whoever it is they are directed at—usually children.

Talking about it is the process of talking about and all around anger but not feeling it (for real, on a completely involved, fully aware level), and of course not conveying the feeling of it. This is usually a more or less completely intellectual process in which *words about* become a substitute for the real thing. The people who make use of this process often know that they are supposed to get angry and act accordingly—but all that comes through is words or play-acting. I remember sitting in a small playground in Brooklyn Heights frequented by young intellectual mothers and their small children. One four-year-old boy threw sand into the eyes of a still-younger little girl. The mother calmly called him over and proceeded to give him a long lecture on playground etiquette and the right and wrong ways of behaving. She delivered her lecture in flat, calm monotones, completely devoid of feeling but excellent in diction and vocabulary. She said, "I am angry," with no effect whatsoever. All in all, it was an excellent lecture on playground ethics delivered by a person obviously well versed in writing college papers, but it conveyed no emotional or affective message at all. The child was bored and restless throughout and was happy to get back to his sand. He learned nothing about anger from her, except perhaps that it was important to deaden and intellectualize it away. She—the mother—went back to reading, obviously content with what she probably considered the height of modern mothering, little aware of her important failure.

By contrast, I am reminded of the story of another four-year-old. This one was "playing" and progressively destroying intricately constructed department store displays while his mother was preoccupied elsewhere. Several salespeople as well as customers attempted to "calm" him with sensible and somewhat intricate lectures and intellectual understanding—all to no avail. They finally called the department-store psychologist. He took the boy aside, whispered a few words in his ear, and as if by magic, the storm was over. One of the salesmen eager to participate in obvious wisdom asked the psychologist what he said. He replied, "I simply said stop upsetting the store, you little——or I'll beat your——off." Obviously, the message was conveyed. The little boy understood—and good relations and peace ensued. Perhaps for the first time, the boy had been told honestly and straightforwardly, with honest respect, within what limits he could operate. This makes for security, since it contributes to a sense of who he is and what he can and can't do.

Acting angry is a poison that does in fact often come from slush and as an effort to do the necessary. But only too often it is an act and nothing more. It does not dissipate anger, and it conveys no message to the recipient other than confusion and sometimes ridicule. An act is an act and is felt as an act and seen as an act and nothing more. Parents are the principal users of this particular poison. They "act" angry, sometimes even working up hysteria because they "know" they "should be angry" even though they don't feel it. Often, they start laughing just when the act seems to be going best. This laughing is really directed at themselves and their obviously ridiculous phony efforts. The child picks it up, too. He feels the confusion and the lack of honesty, and he resents his parents, since he feels correctly that they are being disrespectful to him. Remember, it is hard to fool adults but almost impossible to fool children. They do not respond to what an adult says so much as to what the adult *feels*. An adult—frozen in the angry department—will seem frozen, confused, and confusing, however good an actor he may be.

Bullying

Bullying is a poison even more remote from healthy anger or its exchange or expression than *let's pretend*. Like all arrogant people, the bully feels particularly fragile, vulnerable, and threatened and covers up his feelings of inadequacy by attempting to dominate and derogate others. Bullying can be blatant and obvious or extremely subtle. Bullies have a great talent for picking victims who will tolerate them. They will often form blatant blasting relationships. When they pick the "wrong victim" and genuine anger is turned to them, they almost invariably collapse in panic, having had little or no experience with the real thing.

Some of the most vicious forms of bullying—blatant or subtle—take place between parents and children. This is true of severely neurotic parents who are "don't-make-wavers," as well as those who are obvious despots (however benevolent). The former uses martyrdom and guilt to bully and manipulate; the latter uses superior strength, cunning, and experience and sometimes blatant blasting (overt verbal sadism). Blatant blasting and martyred mothers are described a little later on.

Bullies derive most of the energy necessary for their enterprise from their slush fund. At times they will manage to appear genuinely angry at a genuine hurt, indiscretion, or the like, but careful observation will demonstrate that their anger is synthetic and actually used as a vehicle for the main enterprise, which is to subjugate and to harass their victims.

Bullies are particularly fearful people and as such have a long history of reluctance to feel or to express healthy anger. They are, therefore, guaranteed to have an almost inexhaustible slush fund to use for their bullying needs.

Supersweet Talk

This special little poison is a particularly virulent form of self-effacement and the "nice-guy, don't-make-waves" syndrome. With it, apple-polishing is carried on to a bizarre degree. The victim gets sweeter and sweeter as he gets more and more angry. He is particularly sweet to the person or persons at whom he is angriest. He simply cannot tolerate even the possibility that anyone will get angry at him. His total preoccupation is therefore with those persons who for some reason may get angry at him. These are invariably the persons he likes least and at whom he is angriest. He largely ignores those he likes and trusts. They pose no threat, and he needs all his energy for sweetening up "potential enemies." He thus lives in a topsy-turvy world designed to keep him safe but utterly lacking in happiness or honesty.

Sometimes the victim of this strange poison can be utterly destructive to himself in order to impress someone who couldn't possibly have any effect on, let alone importance in, his life. I remember a woman patient who, after her first few interviews with me, came late just about every visit. I soon learned that the doorman of my building, who was bored and liked to talk, stopped her for a lengthy conversation each time she came to visit me. Not only did she not discourage these conversations, she actually indulged them in an effort to please him. Later it came out that she disliked this man, that she found him boorish and a bore. But the more he irritated her, the more she attempted to sweeten him, thus putting herself in a dilemma because she did not want to displease me with her lateness. In consequence she spent several sessions attempting to sweeten me, too. Eventually, all this came out—along with considerable rage. It was a great relief to her to find out that she wasn't such a sweet thing after all and no longer had to use extraordinary energy and time to maintain the pretense of being something she wasn't. Of course as her poisons became untwisted, she became more honest about herself and others, thus making constructive relationships possible.

"Sweetness" is the order of the day. Sweetness is the big cover-up, and it almost always covers up a huge cesspool of explosive slush, as well as vast sickness in all ways of relating. People who see themselves as "sweet" make a virtue of it: they see themselves as expert cheek-turning missionaries. This myth is destroyed when ample slush explodes to the surface, often producing very serious—and painful—emotional disturbances.

Blatant Blasting

Whenever you are in contact with blatant blasting, you will certainly know it. Sometimes it even looks like the real thing, like the unperverted stuff—real anger born of real feelings. But it is no such thing. Its very strength and chronicity give it away. The blatant blasters are the people who always look as if they are angry. But they don't really feel it. There is actually very little they really do feel in a straight, unperverted way.

What I'm talking about here is verbal sadism, à la *Who's Afraid of Virginia Woolf?* These are people who blatantly blast away. Sometimes they do this with any seemingly willing victim. Sometimes they form li-aisons specially designed for this purpose. There are relationships based on little else than the common need to verbally tear someone down. Karen Horney brilliantly described the dynamics of sadism in various works. Sadists suffer from an inordinate dearth of feelings. They are emotionally dead. They just don't *feel*. Inflicting pain and feeling pain is a last-ditch resort, an attempt at stimulating a feeling of some kind. If they can't evoke feeling in themselves, then evoking pain in others at least vicariously satisfies yearnings to feel. Some blasters like to have an audience; indeed some need and search out an audience. This kind of sadistic exhibitionism has the effect of enlarging the stimulation. This is based largely on the vicarious effect on the audience itself. Blasting, or verbal sadism, is a poison. Blasters are invariably huge slush-fund containers. They above all others are out of touch with their anger. Indeed, as just noted, they are out of touch with all their feelings. By blasting they manage to express some small trace of perverted anger. But the vitriol and acid they spew have little or no relationship to healthy anger. So blasting is a poison, and by blasting, the victim makes use of slush, to stimulate himself and others in an attempt to feel. Unfortunately, the feelings evoked are very paltry and only dimly related to healthy feelings. Momentary feelings of smug satisfaction disappear, leaving an ever-increasing need of the stimulation of more blasting. People trapped in this kind of interplay are invariably involved in very sick ways of relating and in very sick relationships and destructive enterprises.

I remember a woman I eventually treated. She and her husband went to a marriage counselor because their "fights" were badly affecting their young children. The marriage counselor got absolutely nowhere. He did not know that their relationship was based on fighting and that they would resist valiantly any attempt at "peace" or understanding.

So here again is a poison in which things are not the way they seem at all. These hard-hitting, biting, cutting, vindictive people feel very little and are actually very fragile. Sometimes people mistakenly confuse their arrogance as strength (see *The Winners Notebook*—"Strength Weakness Muddle"). Nothing could be further from the truth. Arrogance covers up feelings of emptiness, deadness, lack of self-esteem, and feelings of brittle fragility and vulnerability. Blatant blasting unfortunately further enervates and depletes the victim, removing him still further from constructive relationships, healthy feelings, and potential sources of strength.

Overworking, Oversexing, Overexercising

This is poison that uses the physical approach. Its victims have no idea that they are attempting to "work off feelings." Some have a vague idea of being uncomfortable and then feeling better after "working it off." I am not talking about ordinary work, exercise, or sex (and the range can be great). I'm talking about compulsive overworking, oversexing, overexercising. These, like other compulsive activities, may have multiple causes and can in themselves be evidence of complicated sick attitudes. But I've seen each of these in operation in unconsciously very angry people.

The slush-filled overexerciser seldom engages in merely running it off. Sometimes he becomes somewhat less autistic and will engage in competitive sports, which at least takes on a semblance of communication. I knew one man who played handball and put in extra sessions whenever he felt "out of sorts." He told me how he "murdered the ball" and how he "ran his opponent off the court, worked his ——— off, nearly killed him." He at first made no connection at all between his "out-of-sorts" feelings and feeling very angry. He was eventually able to make the connection when he began to realize that invariably something very irritating had happened before each extra hand-ball session. By the way, this man could ill afford to play at all. He had a bad heart condition. But his kind of self-hating ruthlessness is not unusual among slush-fund exercisers.

Sexual problems abound among large slush-fun-ders. I must say that very few sex problems are pri-mary. They almost always stem from problems in relating to ourselves and others. An individual's sex practices are always a reflection of how he functions and relates generally. Here again, the problems are complex and always reflect many relating difficulties. Indeed this is true of just about all human emotional phenomena. They form an intricate interdependent network so that all emotional upheavals produce repercussions throughout the whole person and his relating life. Just as emotional problems abound in an almost endless variety of combinations and permutations, the same is true of sexual problems. Slush-funders are no exception. They contribute much poison in the area of sex. Many are almost overtly hostile. They manage to tease, excite, and frustrate. Some use their sexual partners in a frozen, mechanical way that is completely devoid of a real relating or emotional experience and lacks every semblance of emotional investment. Some use sex like the handball player—to work off angry feelings, and fatigue themselves in order to become narcotized—all with complete lack of awareness of anger or its perversion. I have had patients whose faces and voices expressed the exact antithesis of "love" as they described the sex act. Some used language that was particularly lacking in evidence of tenderness, warmth, or affection, let alone love. I have known men who "protest" that it is their great love of women that makes them constant questers of "love." Yet these men turn out to want nothing more than mechanical intercourse—*a working off*—and in no way show any sign of affection for women.

Some oversexers have very serious sexual problems, among them great fears of sexual inadequacies and more than the usual fear of homosexuality. (I am not suggesting that too much sexual activity occurs between lovers. The frequency rate varies enormously, and normal bounds are very flexible. I'm talking about a specific condition here, namely, the constant search for mechanical sexual action devoid of anything else. These are the true sex-and-run people.)

Some sex athletes in fact show intense hostility and

real hatred, and among them are those who are overtly sadistic in their sexual practices. Yet with many there is so great an interest vested in keeping their hostility hidden that they are in no way aware of any hostile feelings. When they are confronted with their sadism, the rationalizations abound: "Oh, it's just for variety," "Oh, she likes it," and so on. It is interesting to note here that psychiatric workers have found that a good many male slush-funders have problems with impotency. Many are premature ejaculators. Their unconscious hostility is such that they would prefer (unconsciously) to ejaculate prematurely—making it impossible for coitus to take place—rather than give women any significant satisfaction. I have found that impotence is only one side of slush-fund operations.

Many "frigid women" are also tremendous slush-funders—too full of unconscious hatred to permit letting-go close harmony with another human being to take place. After they resolve their angry problems, closeness, including sexual closeness, often takes place with great satisfaction. Let me say that *healthy adult* sexual activity requires mutual closeness and trust. ("You really care for me" has meaning, as does "I love you.") Slush-funders are in a very poor position for either closeness or trust. They may not know that they are angry, but they are simply not at ease and are never completely themselves in relation to anyone else. This is especially true of sex, which represents the potential for the greatest closeness of all. Therefore it is not at all surprising that the sexual area becomes a poisoned one and that sexual poisons abound.

What about compulsive overworking? Here again there is a boundless variety of psychological dynamics or roots. The particularly large slush-funders who are overworkers are very similar to my handball player. They use working as a way of "working off" all feelings, among them anger. I had one patient who was a very wealthy man but a compulsive worker—to the point of eighteen hours a day. It became more and more apparent as time went on that he funneled all his emotions into and through his work. His total outlook was unilateral—work. He came to see me because his wife threatened to leave him. A few interesting things became apparent. There were times when he described his work lovingly, with great affection. There were other times in which he talked of his work in an almost continuous temper tantrum. (Of course, he seldom talked of anything but work, since this was the absolute-security prison he had built himself.) Eventually it became apparent that in a great majority of instances his anger stemmed from other sources entirely but, as with everything else, he felt his anger only through work. Getting this way (his egomaniacal ambition, his greediness) was of course a long, intricate process, as was his treatment. But for our purposes it is important to know that it became apparent that this man was one of the angriest ever—and he didn't know it. What's more, he had almost never expressed anger at the time or place of its inception or to the person whom he felt might have caused it. It also became apparent that any seeming infraction on the part of his wife was immediately followed by even more work. He was punishing her in this way (with a removal of his presence) but didn't know it. It was a long time before he knew that he had great difficulty being emotionally close to anyone—especially his wife, in his relationship with whom he had the strongest potential feelings.

Savers

Savers are the victims of long-term poison. They are special "don't-make-wavers" who spend a lifetime twisting perverted anger into a cancerous, poisonous smoke screen.

These are the (unconscious and sometimes not-so-unconscious) keepers of permanent gripe lists. They often operate on a supersweet-talk basis, too. In any case, their relationship with people remains an essentially dishonest one. Most savers see themselves, not as enormous gatherers of anger, but rather as beleaguered, misunderstood, "understanding" martyrs. On the basis of this martyrdom, they feel they deserve all kinds of special consideration and undying love. When these aren't forthcoming they feel they have been unjustly treated—and they get angry, turn it off, save it, and feel even more martyred. They are the great injustice collectors. Those that finally come into treatment demonstrate a remarkable memory for every seeming injustice committed against them over a lifetime. Most come into treatment when leakage starts taking place after years and years of saving. An inability to continue to deny anger is felt as terrifying indeed and produces enormous anxiety and depression since it threatens to destroy the entire savings account and the martyred image along with it. Some do not suffer an acute or sudden leak. They manage to save up their anger for twenty years and then slowly leak it out for the next twenty years. When this slow, chronic leakage takes place, it nearly always stems from injustices committed (against the martyred saver) in the past. Savers don't dare deal with present events. This might start an avalanche and a complete flood and inundation. Leakage of the past can bring some relief while the martyred, nonangry, sweet image is still maintained. I remember one woman who sweetly talked about wrongs committed by her husband in the past and how "I always took them" but who invariably managed to end the treatment hour convinced of the sweetness of their relationship—now. Of course she never really had let him know how she felt. Consequently there were many false elements to their relationship—little phony acts, and so on—and at best it had gross limitations. She ostensibly came to see me because of trouble with a daughter. Eventually she realized that her real trouble was with herself and her attitude toward all people. In time she became a much "realer" person. As her slush saving account diminished, she became more self-assertive—with both her husband and her daughter. Relationships in the family improved all around because they were no longer dealing with mirror images and superficially sweet, pleasing shadows. Thus this patient began to deal with real people as the frustration of living incommunicado began to dissipate.

Subtle Sabotage

This poison, unlike self-sabotage, is directly aimed at other people—usually a "loved one," especially a mate. Since it is destructive to important relationships, it, too, must invariably have a self-sabotaging effect. Subtle sabotage varies in degree from very subtle with minor issues to quite blatant with major ones. The recipient of subtle sabotage, or SS, almost always resents being sabotaged and detests the sneak-attack methodology employed. This is its major contribution to ruinous relationships. Of course the sabotage is actually subtle only to the saboteur himself. He must keep it subtle to maintain his unawareness about this form of twisting and poisoning.

Let me give you some examples of SS that I've run into. Remember they range from subtle to not-so-subtle—involving trivial issues as well as issues of relative importance. Some are actually quite ridiculous. But however ridiculous, the effect is always the same—dishonest sneak punches giving no opportunity for comeback.

Always managing to have a laughing or giggling attack when someone just comes to the punch line in telling a joke, when someone is about to make an important point in a discussion, or at particularly sweet or crucial moments during love-making.

Chronic borrowing and neglecting to return things or finally returning them just a bit damaged or the worse for wear.

Chronic forgetting of anything, everything—objects, opportunities, things to be done, and so on. But the forgetting always involves deprivation for another person. I remember a patient who frequently shopped for herself, her husband (who was an extremely busy man), and her children but always forgot something she was supposed to bring home for her husband—a newspaper, an article of clothing, food, etc. She never forgot anything for herself or the children. She simply couldn't understand why he "fussed and fumed so—over such trivia." At one point she refurnished her home and was completely satisfied when the painstaking, long, involved job was done. Imagine her surprise when she suddenly discovered that she "somehow forgot to buy him [her husband] a dresser or a wardrobe."

Insisting on talking during movies, plays, and concerts is another form of SS.

Managing always to bump into people or trip them or spill a little something on them or their prized possessions.

Habitual lateness. This saboteur always keeps you waiting, is always late, breaks appointments the last minute, or simply forgets to come or even arrives the wrong day.

Embarrassing one's companions with inappropriate or loud talk or dress, etc.

Giving misinformation, wrong directions, and poor directions again and again.

Putting all the food on the table but omitting the silverware or the cream for the coffee, butter for the bread, salt, sugar, and so on.

Getting sudden attacks of stupidity. Being unable to understand the clearest, simplest explanations and then not comprehending the recipient's frustration and rage.

Being sexually provocative, teasing and then frustrating.

After starting out on the same side on an issue, suddenly reversing one's stand for no logical reason. I know a physician whose wife was a master of this one. No matter what the discussion was about or who was involved, she always entered it agreeing with her husband. About halfway through she invariably did a complete about-face, ending in support of anyone or everyone who took the position contrary to his. At times "she would forget herself" and instead of merely identifying with her husband's adversary, a potential aggressor (about which more in the next chapter), she herself would become quite vitriolic. During all this she always managed a sweet smile and a low dignified voice. She simply couldn't understand why her husband "took the discussion so seriously" and sometimes ended the discussion in absolute wrath. She was unaware that he felt as though he had been stabbed in the back.

The SS list could of course go on and on. I'm sure you know of many examples. Whatever they are, remember that they are all products of the slush fund and invariably poison one's relationships and one's self.

"I'm with You"

Psychiatrists call this poison "identification with the aggressor." In effect, people poisoned in this way tell themselves—unconsciously—that "If you seem to be aggressive then *I'm with you* and I try to feel some satiation of my own aggressive needs vicariously through you." Here is another way of putting it: "I can't do it, so you do it for me. Neither you nor I will know that you are doing it for me. Your doing it will not involve the right people, the right time, or the right incidents, but maybe I'll derive some benefit anyway." Aggression identifiers are almost always people who live vicariously in other ways, too. They usually steer clear of involvements, big interests, important decisions, and certainly anything that will produce emotional conflicts. These are strictly sideline people. They watch the game being played and they identify with the players, but they never actually enter into the proceedings. At times they may look as if they've made a meaningful move—that is, one that involves a real laying-it-on-the-line or an emotional investment. But investigation will prove otherwise. They sometimes join organizations or causes, but here again their membership remains superficial, mechanical, and aloof. They are there as spectators, their only purpose being vicarious.

The need for aggressors with whom to identify sometimes takes strange forms and produces strange bedfellows. Let me describe several.

There are nice, milquetoasty people who manage to own the most vicious dogs imaginable. This is a case of double identification. The dog picks up his master's unconscious aggressive needs, and the master identifies with the dog's brutality. When the dog attacks someone, the usual statement is "Can't understand it—used to be so gentle—can't understand how he got that way."

There are "pals" who hang around together and who serve each other's purpose. One is aggressive and needs an audience. The other needs an aggressor with whom to identify.

There are persons who will provoke other people into fighting and then will sit as an audience and "watch." There are those otherwise completely passive ladies who go to wrestling matches and yell, "Kill him, kill him, kill him!" I remember one, the sweetest thing you ever saw—surely no slush at all—who saw at least ten boxing matches a year. She had all kinds of rationalizations for it ("It's just the only sport that's easy enough for a dope like me to understand"). This delicate creature actually used to scream, "I want blood, I want blood, let me see blood—blood, blood, blood!"

There are those who will provoke aggression toward themselves. Others wonder why they do it. But they do it time and again, then sit and take it. I had a patient who knew exactly what "buttons to push to turn her husband on." "It's like I push the buttons and turn him on and then just sit there while he really gives me hell. I just don't know what in me pushes me to do it." After months and months of very hard work she found out. She had a considerable fund of slush—of which she was totally unaware. She was much too sweet ever to get angry. The kind of manipulation she used satisfied her masochistic needs, her self-hating needs, her glorious martyrdom, and provided her with an aggressor with whom to identify. The best part of the game was that she could completely hide (from herself) the fact that she got satisfaction from identifying with her husband's aggressive role. After all, how could this be—when she herself was the victim, the very picture of a suffering, martyred, helpless woman? But the truth did out, complicated though it was. She eventually realized that she "pushed the buttons" or manipulated the situation. She used her husband to make her a *victimized martyr* as well as to provide her with *vicarious aggression* to satisfy sadistic needs, which she wanted to keep absolutely hidden from view since they did not fit in with her long-standing, sweet self-image. She also came to realize that she was a very angry woman who had perverted her anger for years and had twisted it into many poisons.

There are people whose desperate need will make them use anyone at all who even seems aggressive. They will do this for short or long periods of time—in fleeting acquaintanceships (at social discussions), in sustained relationships, and with utter strangers (a brawl in a bar, or have you seen adults watch one child really hurt another in a street fight while they just stand there and look on?). I remember one man who could not have been more milquetoasty than he was. He had been born in Europe and had come to America in his early twenties and spoke with a very heavy Russian-Yiddish accent. Periodically, his accent would become Westernized, sort of a cowboy Jewish-Russian accent. He'd also use words like "partner," "tote," and so on. He would do this usually for a week or ten days, and then he'd revert to straight Russian-Yiddish-English. I finally found out that Mr. S. loved cowboy movies, and I was going to let it go at that. But on further investigation it came to light that he saw the bloodiest Westerns and came out feeling like one of the cowboys. He said he even found himself swaggering a little as if he had just got off a horse (he never rode one in his life) and it all felt "sort of nice." The cowboy he identified with in any film was not necessarily either the hero or the villain. He was always simply "the big doer—the *tough* guy."

I had a young woman in a group-treatment situation who was easily the most passive member of the group. But she was always on the side of the person who was the most aggressive in any given session. Of course this deprived her of any chance to tap her own self and to see what she really felt or thought. Unfortunately she was used to this kind of self-neglect. Then when some of her group began to notice that her ordinarily impassive face actually lit up and became animated whenever aggression (on the part of others) was expressed, they confronted her with the fact, and she, too, realized that she "got a kick" out of what was going on: "I guess I like to see someone really dish it out." This realization eventually opened the door to some very important insights on her part.

Another form this poison takes, which I briefly mentioned before, is joining various groups. Some young people will join gangs in order to identify with potential aggression. Some persons are chronic, indiscriminate joiners of protest organizations. Some don't really care what is being protested. Some switch sides at the drop of a hat largely to be on the most aggressive side. Some "very passive people" (but think of what their slush funds must be like) find themselves in the center of a mob action with no idea of how they got there. Some men find they have joined the army ". . . but how? Just had a drink and heard this hard-hitting recruiting sergeant." Still others are policemen for years and swear that they are incapable of real aggression. This is not hard to understand when we realize that "I'm with you" almost always takes place on a completely unconscious level. The individual so poisoned does not know that he is identifying with an aggressor, potential aggressor, or aggression.

There is a peculiar but extremely important derivation of this poison that sometimes takes place between parents and children. Remember that I said earlier that children are extremely well tuned in to what their parents feel. They are superb observers. They are often tuned in to their parents' unconscious desires even though the parent may know nothing of those desires. When a parent says "Don't do this" or "No!" and means it, the child knows the parent means it. But when the parent says no (because it's the thing to say in a particular issue) but really feels yes, the child knows this, too. He picks up the difference in voice tone, the difference in gesture, the fleeting little smile at the corner of a mouth, or the raised eyebrow—all of which the parent cannot control and is unaware of. Indeed the child may not "know" they exist either. That is, he may not know on a conscious, thinking level. But deep down where it counts and where he feels and where he is motivated to action, he *knows*. Therefore, there are many children (by no means all) who in fact are responding to a parent's unconscious desires for aggression and to a parent's unconscious desires to identify with his or her children and to live vicariously through them. The roots of sociopathy and social delinquency are very complicated, and this dynamic certainly does not account for all cases. But it is a very important factor in many of them. With young people—particularly those who live at home—treatment avails nothing unless the parent is treated, too.

Response to a seemingly passive parent's unconscious aggressive needs can be subtle or blatant, minor or major. We have all seen mothers who visit someone's house—perhaps yours—and let a small child slowly but surely destroy whatever is in his reach with no effort to control him or with an effort so puny as to effect an endorsement of what he is doing. Unfortunately, not all cases are this trivial (however annoying). There are boys who will commit multiple antisocial aggressive acts (who have the most "peace-loving parents in the world"). As the chief psychiatrist of the Women's House of Detention, Department of Correction of New York City, I saw a considerable number of "sexual acter-outers." Occasionally a girl would come from a home where sex couldn't have been handled on a more Victorian level. Of course parents with enormous sexual repressions often also have strong unconscious needs to break out and to act out something, which children sometimes "do for them." For some people sexual acting-out or promiscuity and prostitution are intimately linked to aggressive needs and are a way of fighting authority. The authority in such cases may seem to be law or society or the Establishment, but the aggression may actually be displaced from the tyrannical, repressive, overrestrictive, constrictive, overburdening conscience of a parent or parents. Of course there are many conditions, possibilities, and complications. However subtle, perverted anger and all the poisons are always terribly destructive to human relations. In this particular form of "I'm with you" some of the destructive possibilities in the all-important parent-child relationship can be disastrous.

Half-Poisons

There are two principal types of sneak-attack half-poisons—poison-pen letters and hitting and running. I call these half-poisons because there is a modicum of real anger that is felt and discharged—even transmitted. But unfortunately these, too, are stunted versions of the real thing.

There is certainly nothing wrong in writing letters as a means of communicating real anger. It is not quite up to being there in person, but it can accomplish quite a lot in its own way. However, this in no way applies to anonymous letters. The anonymous writer is always suffering from one or another form of emotional disturbance, which is usually revealed by the content of the letter. Some of these letters are not even subtle: there are those that are obviously sadistic and grotesque. But what about the *writing* of these letters, regardless of content—I mean the *process of writing* any poison-pen letter? This is a poison, first, because it is nearly always generated, not by a single event or act, but rather by the whole slush fund. It is only the slush fund that can generate and sustain the pressure necessary to produce the motivation to write these letters. But it is more than that. The writer does not really accept his stand and does not stand behind it. He is actually ashamed of it and refuses to affix his name to and to identify with it. And there is an even more destructive aspect here. The poison-pen writer has no desire to communicate or to relate. He wants only to hurt and to feel himself the master of his stabbing missive. His goal has nothing to do with the purposes involved in communicating healthy anger. He is not interested in the recipient's feelings, thoughts, or explanations. He is not interested in clearing the air, improving understanding, or bettering relations. If anything, he wants to maintain his hostility (more about hostility versus anger in the next chapter), his own bad feelings, and the bad feelings he hopes to produce in others.

The hit-and-runner, though usually not as sadistic in his intent as the poison-penner, functions largely in the same way. He, too, kills off any possibility of meaningful, constructive emotional interchange. He, too, leaves his victim frustrated and unable to make a proper rejoinder—which is sometimes part of his conscious purpose and sometimes is unconscious. The hit-and-runner does just what the name implies. After first making sure that he can run—and I mean fast—he hits with some kind of twisted angry barb and then runs. Perhaps you've heard the typical statement: "Sorry, I'd really like to hear you out but must go." The hit-and-runner is very often a touch-and-go person generally. His relating consists mainly of small, superficial contacts rather than sustained emotional involvements. Thus he hits and runs in all ways, socially, emotionally, and often professionally as well. He simply doesn't stay around with the whole of himself long enough to be anything more than a dilettante socially, emotionally, or professionally.

"Don't Worry
About Me"

This is a particular kind of poison that at one and the same time is used in a combined attempt to discharge venom, disarm the victim, and manipulate him. The poison manipulators never admit to themselves or anyone else that any of these things are true. They will look upon the recipient of their venom as absolutely crazy if he so much as mentions the possibility that hostility is being directed toward him. A poison manipulator is usually a genius at timing and wording. She or he also usually has the added benefit of years of experience and generally knows the victim extremely well. Very commonly the manipulator is the victim's mother. Her hostile manipulations have been going on as part of a long continuum. Let me give you a typical example.

A young man is about to go with his sweetheart.

His mother (Mau Mau in this case) says to him as a parting shot just as he's about to step out of the house, "You shouldn't worry about me while you are out with that person having a good time. Believe me, I want you to have a good time. Lately, my balance isn't so good. Happens to old people—it's nothing. But if I fall down the stairs while you are gone, don't worry. Even with a broken hip I can still reach the phone and call the doctor. So have a good time, please!"

The attempt here is to manipulate her son not to go out. Chances are that there is a long history of maternal possessiveness and an attempt at living vicariously through the boy. Obviously there is jealousy of "that person"—his sweetheart—whom she derogates by calling her neither by name nor by gender. There is slush hostility (the form here is manipulative poison) directed at both young people in an attempt to spoil their good time by trying to manufacture and instill worry and guilt. If confronted with any of this, the mother will say, "Are you crazy? You have a mother complex or something? I should spoil your good time? Me hostile to you? This word *hostile*—lately everybody is hostile? Some hostile—your mother who only lives for you."

Of course she is unaware and must go on denying. Since she herself uses guilt as a weapon, she is not about to use it on herself. Besides, the idea of hostility would destroy her image of perfect and ever-devoted motherhood. But even in her protest she is still consistently manipulative and hostile and still attempting to engender guilt. "Your mother who only lives for you" is an extremely hostile statement. In effect it says, "I give my life for you, therefore you owe me yours. Nothing you do for me is enough. You are in debt to me and can never pay off that debt. Remember, your own life is not your sole responsibility. You have to worry about mine also."

Easy Talk

Easy talk is malicious gossip. The only thing easy about it is the way people gently slip in and out of this vicious enterprise, often with no awareness at all. This poison is obviously destructive to all concerned—to the talker, to the listeners, and potentially to the subject. It represents twisting slush and unfortunately is almost never linked with hostility in the mind of the talker. The easy talker more often than not has one other (other than to twist and rid himself of perverted poison) reason to convey malice through gossip. He usually easy talks in order to be liked. Of course his easy talk usually makes him despised, but he doesn't know this when he starts out. How can he feel that gossip will lead to being liked? Unconsciously or possibly with some small awareness, he feels that he is bestowing gifts upon his listeners. After all, isn't he letting his listeners in on confidential, secret, and potentially destructive information? He is not only sharing great treasures with them but is also providing them with entertainment through stimulation and excitement. Isn't he giving them material to pique the imagination? For this he expects to be liked and admired. This puts him (he thinks) in a position of power and prestige. So he feels that he can have his cake and eat it, too. He has discovered the perfect comprehensive stratagem: just quietly slip into loose, easy talk and he can give vent to slush, be liked, and achieve social power. All these effects exist only in his own imagination. Gossip, much like envy and jealousy, exacts its corrosive toll on the easy talker and his relationships. People, especially healthy ones, do not exactly become endeared to gossips. Indeed, relationships with mature people are inevitably destroyed by easy talk.

Auto Poison

Auto poison is not carbon monoxide. Auto poison is the very special but deadly stuff found throughout the world which chronic car-accident makers use to kill and maim other people and themselves. I feel very strongly that many automobile accidents are not accidental at all. The chronic auto killer may not be aware of any hostile intent, but his chronicity in this matter is evidence of unconscious intent. Slush is the fuel, the automobile is the weapon, and the results are only too obvious. Of course people who cause accidents may also suffer from a multiplicity of emotional difficulties, but the principal stuff of auto poison is perverted anger. How often we see a so-called nice, easygoing guy become omnipotently maniacal on the road. He is full of auto poison, and he is spewing it out all over the highway. On the road he is anonymous, just another driver, and he needn't fear any assault on his nice-guy status. But he and his car are one, and together they become a formidable instrument of vengeance. On the road they can strike out for every bit of hurt pride ever experienced. Together they can attempt to exact vindictive triumph for every seeming wrong ever inflicted on Mr. Nice Guy. That he doesn't know his enemy (other cars and drivers) makes it so much easier for him to switch to them all kinds of feeling about other people (from home, for example). What's more, he can go on being ostensibly peace loving. How much easier to work out sibling rivalry, feelings of sexual inadequacy, inability to stand up to the boss or to a castrating wife or mother—and all the anger these produce—on the well-populated road where he is anonymous. I feel very strongly that a great many automobile accidents occur because persons suffering from much perversion of anger, from bursting slush funds, bring it to cars and roads, where it overflows.

Telling the Truth

Telling the truth can be a virtue, but the particular motive involved is all-important. I am speaking of a form of "sneak speaking." I mentioned truth-telling in describing "but people" in the chapter on Talk, Talk, Talk, and No Talk. They use truth as an excuse for slipping a barb in here and there.

"Telling the truth," however, is a primary kind of poison used by some people. They invariably look for particular truths that will hurt. They are not interested in truths that will enhance the recipient's self-esteem, that will make for feeling good, that will be supporting or comforting. Somehow the truths they find will be linked to bad memories, skeletons in the closets, fears, and hurts. When they run out of these, they will distort, exaggerate, and often lie. They do so because for all their "truth-telling," they are not particularly honest people. Hostility is in no way to be equated with honesty. Of course they will deny distorting, subtle lying, and especially blatant lying (this denial is also a form of lying). How can they admit to lying? Such an admission would uncover and link them to their true intent—namely, to hurt, to cause pain, to tear down, to maim. It would link them to their slush fund—which is threatening to "nice-guy stuff." Remember they use "truth" as the biggest lie of all. "Truth" is their big rationalization, their big cover-up for intense hostility. Under the guise of "truth" they are able to deny being angry, they are able to continue playing their "nice-guy" role, and they can even seem to be particularly virtuous—virtually steeped in honesty. I have had patients like this, and I am now particularly wary when an individual spends much time attempting to convince me of his honest and enormous interest in truth. Of course it is quite a shock for these people to find out that they are often blatant and vicious liars—even more so than easy talkers (gossips). But at least this exposure is the first step toward real honesty (with which they can discover what ails them), toward real feelings (especially angry ones), and toward real health.

Spread It Around

In this form of poison, anger is perverted and twisted so that it is felt in every and all conceivable ways except as anger. Sometimes the individual employing this multiple-outlet device will come close to feeling anger as such, but he usually doesn't quite make it.

I am reminded of one patient I had who emerged from anger-producing situations feeling tired, excited, hungry, funny, warm, sick, and so on, but never angry. After a good deal of work, her feelings changed and came closer to being appropriate. In the same kinds of anger-producing situations she said, "I feel rejected, hurt, insulted, stepped on." She still refused to admit that she was actually angry. When I provoked her and a little anger as anger without decoration managed to seep out, she telephoned me at least ten times to apologize and to reassure herself that I still liked her. This was a projection of her own self-rejection as an "angry person." It took many months before she could accept her anger—let alone its expression through other than multiple devious routes.

"Someone Dies"

Dreams can be a form of poison. This is true for individuals whose sole angry outlet is dreams and who continually have dreams that are slush-laden. Dreams are exceedingly complicated psychological manifestations, and their interpretation is a complex business. Many volumes have been written on the subject, and the last word is far from said. All psychoanalysts agree, however, that a dream can be meaningful only in the terms of the dreamer himself. This means that it is necessary to know the history of the dreamer and the particular and individual meaning of his particular symbols (the words and pictures that appear in his dreams). We must approach any kind of generalization or general symbol-meaning with great care. Every analyst, however, is aware that certain kinds of dreams appear again and again in people with big angry troubles. These dreams are obviously slush-fund derivations.

The dreams I speak of here are dreams replete with violence, manifestations of horror, panic, running away, "burying something," "always—someone dies," people disappearing or getting lost or hurt or sick or being killed or getting into terrible trouble or being on trial, and so on. These dreams are often manifestations of great rage and desire for vindication and revenge. Some of the most violent dreams (like peculiar thoughts) are the exaggerated snowball results of what started out as relatively small irritations. Many dreamers forget their dreams and start remembering them only after psychoanalytic treatment has begun. Most angry dreamers will have all kinds of angry associations with the dreams but then will resist linking the dream to anger and will deny feeling angry at all.

I remember a particular patient whose associations were typified by this: "My mother told my friend the very thing I asked her not to tell her. She always does this. No state secrets or anything like that, but I wish she wouldn't do it. Funny thing, last night I dreamed she was dying—my mother. Woke up feeling awful. Me angry at her? No, I don't feel angry. I really love her very much, you know." Interestingly, this particular patient suffered from a psychosomatic condition sometimes found in this kind of killing-mama dream. The patient was a teethgrinder and as a result had a rather serious periodontal condition necessitating much gum treatment.

With some people, dreaming does not offer enough relief and there is an overflow into the waking hours. Many are embarrassed by enormously hostile fantasies in which a loved one or a close friend is suddenly dying, being torn apart, crushed, and so on. This is a relatively common kind of peculiar thought, the result of the distortion and snowballing of repressed anger. When these thoughts are close to a truthful revelation, they sometimes produce panic, which may lead the way to treatment. Hostile fantasies and dreams both tend to disappear as the individual learns to handle anger realistically and effectively. The patient inevitably learns, among other things, that love and anger are not mutually exclusive and that it is quite normal to get angry at loved ones. But more about this in Part 4.

Always Tired

In this chapter I'm not talking about being a little tired. I'm talking about a special psychosomatic effect of slush. This is chronic, severe fatigue. The victim of this poison does not suffer from anemia or any other kind of chemical imbalance. People with this poison are always very tired because they use their entire bodies to ward off anger or any show of it. They go about in a chronic state of great nervous and muscular tension. In effect, they use their bodies much more than anyone else does. They don't know that they are doing this, but nevertheless they are under constant physical pressure. It is as if they have routed all their angry feelings to their muscles, which they must now keep in a constant semicontractual state lest any anger break out and show. Some of these people actually look very tight. I know one man whose jaws always hurt from chronic clenching. It was almost as if he had to keep his jaws closed tight lest the real truth somehow emerge in an unguarded moment. The fatigue here is not imagined. It is very real indeed. Just imagine how tired you would be if you kept your body in a constant state of censored, guarded tension. Interestingly, some of the victims of this poison complain of severe cramping in various muscles, and some have been treated for "poor circulation." I know one man who used to chew a hole through a pipe stem at least once a week—until much of his tension and anger were rerouted through healthier channels.

Joking and Boring

Many books have been written about humor, and much time and space have been devoted to the relationship between humor and hostility. A sense of humor is most certainly a very valuable asset. To be able to laugh at one's self and at one's troubles, without contempt, can even be lifesaving. But I'm talking here about a different kind of joking. I'm talking about a very serious poison that is comprised almost entirely of perverted anger. I'm talking about compulsive joking, a chronic form of joking that never stops. It frustrates, it bores, and it keeps people at a distance. Indeed, the compulsive joker cannot get serious even when someone else's life depends on it.

Many of the compulsive joker's "jokes" are anything but funny. Some are thinly veiled statements conveying extreme hostility. For the most part, they are blatantly personal, bigoted, vicious, vulgar, often disgusting, and always destructive. They are designed to sneak in and dissipate enormous rage under the guise of entertainment and good fellowship. They are always the antithesis of either warm, healthy humor or warm, healthy anger. More often than not, they are a crashing bore, and the boredom itself is a very effective form of vindictive hostility. Indeed, the compulsive joker who is running out of jokes may turn to the poison blood brother—boring. I feel that chronic bores—people who insist on telling you personal details of their lives or things that you already know and they know you know—are actually engaging in a form of torture. Compulsive jokers are particularly good at this form of torture through boredom.

I remember one patient who was a compulsive joker. After we worked on this awhile, he switched to boring. When I pointed this out, thus cutting off another poison outlet, he had quite a reaction. Real hot anger was spewn all over the place—undiluted and undisguised. This was followed by tears, then relief, then real hard work on some very important personality problems. This kind of reaction is understandable when one considers the enormous amount of slush— just beneath the surface—necessary to keep a chronic jokester joking and boring.

Phony Peace

This is an insidious poison found among "don't-make-wavers" who are often also supersweet talkers. These are people who want peace at any price and who often pay an enormous price to get it. The price is often equal to complete self-effacement or destruction of self. They simply turn themselves into fragmented mirrors—reflecting what they think everyone else wants. In the process they lose themselves—that is, their own true feelings and identities. They never appear angry. This would disturb the "peace." But they are laden with slush, and the principal poison they twist slush into is phony peace. I say *phony* because it isn't real peace at all. It's almost always a thin patch of sweet words that covers enormous intrafamilial tensions, rages, and misunderstandings. If people are quiet in this kind of household, it is only because they are afraid that if they talk, the truth will out and it will be a very angry and turbulent truth indeed.

Victims of this particular poison invest enormous energy keeping and believing in peace. Of course real peace can never exist unless the air is really cleared—something these people dread. Indeed, they will deny its necessity, since no one in this household ever gets angry or unpeaceful. If anyone does get angry the others usually rationalize it away with statements like, "Oh, he's not angry, just a little enthusiastic, that's all." No amount of saccharin and solicitude fools anyone who is operating on any kind of reality basis. These are usually the children in the house, who feel that they are living with emotional time bombs. This makes children feel extremely insecure, tense, confused, and anxious. Parents often can't understand these manifestations inasmuch as their children have been provided with such a "peaceful household—never a shout or harsh word."

"I'm So Sick"

This poison takes several forms, ranging from the relatively benign to the severely malignant. Severe hypochondriasis is a very malignant form of emotional disturbance which invariably has many roots. Perverted anger converted into anxiety is nearly always a very important component.

Little children often have sick and dying fantasies in order to "get even." "I'll be sick and suffering and dying, and you will all be standing around my bed wringing your hands—and, boy, will you be sorry." Unfortunately many adults use this form of poison not only for its hostile effect but to manipulate in an attempt to get what they want. There are women who feel "sick" unless they get what they want. This sickness takes the form of "heart pains," "dizzy spells," "shortness of breath," "sick headaches," "heart flutters," and the like. There are others who can't have sex because they feel "too sick" or "too tired." This is a sometimes unconscious and at other times a relatively conscious way of punishing their husbands by means of sexual deprivation. Sexual manipulation, however well rationalized by feigned sickness, invariably has disastrous results on a marriage. Straightforward anger and its proper display would be ameliorative indeed.

But what about the person who really thinks that he is sick? The hypochondriac, unlike the individual who has a psychosomatic illness, has no physical lesion. But he does in fact believe that he has a definite illness, and this delusion is his principal psychiatric symptom. Very often this symptom—imagined illness—represents the investment of much buried rage. This imagined illness is a way of coping with perverted anger as well as with great anxiety. Unfortunately it is a very poor way of coping, since the symptom itself is often terribly incapacitating. Its victims are often so completely preoccupied with bodily involvement and sickness that they have little or no energy or time or room in their lives for relating or functioning. Of course any suggestion that they are angry or anxious about something that has nothing to do with their imagined sickness is met with utter disdain. The feeling is, "How can you talk of superficial things like anger and anxiety when I'm probably dying of a terrible disease? The only thing I'm anxious about is that disease. If I were sure I didn't have it, then I would be all right." No amount of reassurance or logic convinces them they don't "have it." How can they, when they desperately need the belief in illness to cover up real and actual problems as well as feelings, among them unwanted slush?

I had one patient who was a very severe hypochondriac. She managed to function on a very superficial basis. The major part of her emotional life, however, was turned inward and focused on her various organs and their possible disfunction. She had intermittent difficulties with her mother, and each time she was irritated with her mother (toward whom she denied feeling angry), she plagued her husband to take her to doctors for reassurance concerning imagined ills. She thus covered up her anger at her mother by concentrating on her ills. She also drove her husband and the doctor to distraction, sometimes calling them twenty times a day. She thus displaced much of her rage from her mother to her husband and to her doctor, as well as to her organs. I refused to reassure her or to talk about her physical ills. If I had, she would have felt that I, too, could be manipulated, and I would have become useless to her. I insisted on talking about what to her seemed superficial—namely, her anger and the ways of handling it—as well as the history of her relationship with people, especially her mother. This was the only way to drain her slush fund and to undermine her symptoms.

Forevermore

There is a form of sustained temper tantrum that simply goes on and on and on. Its victims can't seem to let go of an issue. Sometimes they vent their spleen and seem to have it out of their system, then they begin to remember and start all over again, working up to the same height of rage over and over. Thus when they get angry, they seem to get angry forevermore. I think that this kind of poisonous reaction stems from two principal sources—one purely emotional, the other with possible organic implications. I think the emotional one represents displaced slush-fund drainage. It doesn't matter what the issue is, but each issue taps the slush fund and is sustained until that particular slush-fund compartment is finally drained.

There are a group of people with no outward manifestation of brain damage whose angry responses are sometimes very peculiar. Some of them sustain anger almost forever, never being able finally to close an issue. Others have momentous, uncontrollable tantrums in which great damage is done. These tantrums sometimes take place on an unconscious level (the person has amnesia for the period during which they occur) and can result in uncontrollable murder. This condition when very severe is sometimes indicative of a form of epilepsy. It may or may not be related to the usual angry problems. People who suffer from this condition sometimes do demonstrate abnormal brain waves on the electroencephalogram as well as abnormal findings on physical-neurological (reflexes, etc.) examinations. This unfortunate but rare condition is known as psychomotor equivalents, which means that in lieu of the usual type of convulsive epileptic attack, the victim suffers great motor (muscular movement) activity or an acting out that resembles a huge temper tantrum. If there is no adequate history, it is sometimes necessary to differentiate between this condition and catatonic excitement, which I discussed earlier under "Mutism." Some of the victims of this condition have been wrongly convicted of committing murder and inflicting physical damage when they had neither control nor awareness.

Poison Poisons:
Drugs

Drugs prudently prescribed certainly have a place in psychiatry, though I believe that their value has been exaggerated. They can be used to relieve anxiety, but they do not resolve problems, change attitudes, or effect growth.

But our interest here is drugs as poison and used as a means to further subvert anger, thus creating more slush for poison. I have seen a number of people in consultation who have used narcotics, tranquilizers, energizers, hypnotics, psychedelics, and marijuana in at attempt to escape unwanted feelings. I had one woman as a patient who came to me with a very severe barbiturate habit. She could not sleep unless she took very large doses of Nembutal. She was able to give up the drug only when she became aware that she was chronically intensely angry at her husband and was able to accept and express this anger. She had had no idea consciously that she was angry, let alone that she was attempting to narcotize her anger with drugs. Many drug-users are people who are unconsciously very angry and who confuse their anger with lack of love or antilove. Drugs do not add to one's ability to love. Quite the contrary, they produce isolated distorted reveries that have an autistic effect and are destructive to any process, including love, which necessitates emotional exchange or caring. Drugs used to anesthetize feelings and anxiety further remove the individual from what he feels and who he is. They block important pathways to true and real feelings and destroy the possibility of discovery and growth.

I have repeatedly found that users of psychedelics and marijuana were particularly angry, anxiety-ridden people who were attempting to feel more comfortable with themselves. Anesthetizing powerful feelings does not make for sustained comfort, equilibrium, peace, brotherly love, or constructive purpose. Feelings must out: they must be realized, accepted, expressed, and integrated as part of the whole human being if sustained human growth and worthwhile emotional encounters and exchanges are to take place. Drugs are temporary escapes and provide blocks and pitfalls to the possibilities of human growth. Reality includes reality about one's feelings, whatever they are. To feel—to be oneself—is a reality essential to human progress. Drugs used indiscriminately are the enemy and antithesis of *feeling* reality.

Juice-Stewing

"Juice-stewing," or stewing in one's juice, sometimes takes place individually and very often between two people. More often than not it is a direct function of the pride deadlock (which I discussed in *The Winner's Notebook*). This poison is in a way a milder version of the catatonic reaction. Of course there's a vast difference in degree and quality, too. The victim of this poison knows that he's angry. How can he avoid knowing it: he's seething with rage. *But* he isn't going to let anyone else know it. This would hurt his pride. So he is caught in a pride deadlock, and he forces himself to sit and stew even to the point of inner corrosion. I remember one man who said, "I felt my guts rotting out—I could have busted—but I'd be damned if I'd say anything and give her or anyone else the satisfaction. I'm not going to let her know that she can have that much effect on me." Pathetically, he was so expert that his wife often had no idea of what he was feeling. He would stew and suffer for days and even weeks and all to no avail. His anger was not transmitted, communication was not improved, and he would be set up for self-stewing all over again in a very short time.

The pride deadlock, however, very often involves two people—each stewing in his own particular juice and both intent in maintaining their pride and not telling the other of their rage. I had a patient who used to maintain this condition with her husband for literally months at a time. Unlike others that I've known, these people did speak to each other. But the unwritten rules called for a minimum of grunts and short words about the necessities of life exclusively. They also had unwritten agreements (developed over years) about which parts of the house and its equipment (radio, TV) each had control over. They both prided themselves that neither sounded off, cleared the air, explained, or apologized. They simply lived in an armed camp (sometimes for as long as half a year) until the self-corrosive stew somehow dissipated (inadvertently and probably because of accumulated fatigue and boredom). Neither of these people understood why their children grew up to be very nervous since (they said) they provided them with all the necessities of life. Breaking the pride-deadlock mechanism and destroying juice-stewing are not easy. They entail a complete reexamination of one's life, attitudes, and values. While very constructive, this process can be quite painful. Unfortunately many people are not willing to undergo it until their marriage, their children, and themselves are on or over the brink of disaster.

Slush-Fund
Explosions

Violence—suicide, murder, war—these are the slush-fund explosions. These are the wages of the total breakdown in communications between self and others. These are the results of the failure of words to convey feelings, dissatisfactions, and misunderstandings so that remedial steps can be taken. These are the results of multitudinous accumulated hurts and their distortion and perversion. These are the results of the manufacture of unbridgeable gaps between members of the same species. These are the results of human bridges destroyed by the inability to communicate angry feelings in healthy ways.

Self-destruction, or the annihilation of others, requires psychotic energy. Individual murder and mass murder require psychotic energy. Illegal murders by "mad-bombers" or "sneak snipers" and legal murders by state executioners and soldiers in war require psychotic energy. Slush funds provide this energy. Twisting provides the process of converting this energy into the psychotic process of maiming and killing. Killing is never the result of love of either an individual, a cause, or a country. It is never the result of healthy interest or passion. Healthy members of the same species do not willfully hurt themselves or their brothers. Killing is the sick result of hurt neurotic pride—be it individual, mass, or national pride. Violence is the antithesis of healthy angry feelings and expressions. Its message is remote from that conveyed by anger. Its object is never increased understanding and growth but rather sickness and stagnation. Its malignant children are humiliation, horror, misery, pain, vengeance, and death. "I'll kill you a hundred times" is a statement made in jest. But to some people it is not jest. They feel that a thousand killings would only begin to relieve them of their enormous stockpile of hatred.

Will glory one day be measured in terms of increased understanding and better communication? Will military parades give way to penicillin parades?

Short Circuits

This is at one and the same time the sum total of all the poisons plus the total poisonous effect.

The poisons do not function in isolation. They are not mutually exclusive. As a matter of fact, they are almost always found operating in symbiotic destructive partnerships. Some of us use one poison more than others, but if our angry outlook and outlets are sick, then we shall surely use several of them. The total effect is always the same. They produce short circuits in the lines of human communication. They alienate us from our own feelings, and they alienate us from our fellows. These short circuits produce further poisonous effects on how we feel about our feelings—particularly anger. In this way multitudinous vicious circles are established that continue to damage many possibilities of realizing untapped resources, as well as potentially rewarding, honest relationships. Honest relationships and the rewards which they offer are simply not possible when we function as emotional amputees.

4

UNTWISTING: PROPHYLAXIS AND ANTIDOTES

Perverting and twisting are due largely to fear and prejudice. Here, as elsewhere, fear and prejudice are largely a function of learned misinformation and confusion.

Arresting, preventing, and reversing these processes requires insight about the basic stuff we are dealing with—here, anger.

In this part of The Angry Book *let us take a fresh and healthy look at this all-important human phenomenon and its ramifications.*

What Is It?

We could but we won't go into a long discussion here about biochemical changes in blood-vessel size, normal physiological responses, nerve-fiber responses, and the like. We leave that to the physiologists and biochemists. Our interest is the emotional area—where major difficulty takes place.

Anger can be defined as a universal human response in which a person is aware of being (or feeling) in a state of displeasure. It occurs only in living creatures, and in people, it is replete with feelings of warmth and aliveness. As a matter of fact it *is* warmth and aliveness. It can be accompanied by physical feelings and changes—blood rushing to the face (blushing), quickening heartbeat, and so on. There may be a concomitant desire to yell out, to use strong words, to wave one's hands or arms, and to let others know how one feels. It is an effective (emotional) response and can produce the transmission of an affective and effective message. This can be followed by a give-and-take, mutual exchange of emotional information. In health it is self-limiting. This means that it takes place and then stops. It is often a response to frustration due to misunderstanding. We human beings have a great need to understand one another, very limited ways of transmitting understanding, and exceedingly limited frustration tolerances. This combination guarantees angry responses.

Black and White

Anger is not a black-or-white, all-or-nothing feeling or response. This sounds obvious, but many people feel otherwise. They feel that any feeling or show of anger is tantamount to loss of control and is the same as a huge, uncontrollable temper tantrum. They regard this as a sinful and dangerous misdeed—a strike against one's self—and as potentially dangerous, to say the least. Of course this isn't true. Intensity of anger may vary from the mildest irritation to very powerful feelings and transmissions. There are innumerable shades and nuances. Mild feelings of irritation are hardly the equivalents of uncontrollable rage. Indeed, angry responses very, very seldom reach uncontrollable levels. When they do, they are invariably slush-fund hemorrhages and have little or nothing to do with the immediate irritating situation on hand. People can and do get mildly, moderately, and even intensely angry without loss of control. Actually, the greater their awareness—that is, the closer they are to what they really feel—the less chance there is to lose control. Please remember that loss of control or rationale is due mainly to slush-fund explosions. This kind of response is due mainly to perverted and unconscious anger and has little or nothing to do with the healthy product (regardless of intensity), of which there is always full awareness and possession. To put it another way: our feelings control us when we subvert them and are no longer aware they exist. They then have an autonomy of their own. When we know what we feel, when our feelings are integrated as parts of the whole of us, then regardless of their intensity, we remain completely in charge of ourselves and of all our feelings—as part of a central autonomy.

Feel and Tell

There is a difference between feeling angry, letting one's self in on it, and letting someone else in on it, or making them the recipient of it. The important thing is to know and to accept angry feelings. This in itself will mitigate perverting and the accumulation of slush. Acceptance, real acceptance of angry feelings, without harsh judgment or moral equivocation, combined with the ability to express the anger, will then make possible a choice regarding its expression. Acceptance of feelings plus freedom to express those feelings gives one the chance to decide (choice) whether one wishes or does not wish to express those feelings.

I have had a number of patients with angry troubles who in effect echoed the following remark of a woman I treated: "Supposing I find out that I'm angry with my mother—and that I have been angry for years—what do I do? She's now eighty years old—do I let her have it? She would not understand an iota of what I'm talking about at this point." After this patient worked out her angry problems and really accepted her ability to get angry and her angry feelings, and after she found the ability to convey her feelings to others, she had a choice and made her own decision. She decided that she no longer had the need to convey her feelings to her mother and that it was possible to dissipate them without sharing them with her mother. The all-important change that occurred was that she was now in charge and in a position of decision, since she was no longer alienated from her own feelings.

Timing

The patient I mentioned above—let's call her Irene—also found out that timing is very important. She came to realize that the most effective *affective messages* are delivered at the time of stimulation or disgruntlement—when we get angry. Telling someone how we feel loses effect as times goes on. The message also loses authenticity with time—as issues become distorted and clouded. She also noticed a timing change as she changed. Two processes took place. First, the time between the occurrence of an irritating event and her knowing that she was angry grew shorter and shorter until there was no time lapse at all. Second, Irene realized that the time between her feeling angry and her responding to it with a verbal message became shorter and shorter and eventually nil. In time she knew she was angry as soon as she was angry and was able to express her anger at once if she so chose.

Who

Irene learned something else, too. She realized that we generally get angry at people who have some meaning for us. This applies especially to people who have the capacity to remind us of ourselves and our problems. These are often people who have the same or similar problems. These are almost invariably people who know us and whom we know. We are more likely to get angry at people with whom we relate than those we have nothing to do with.

She also learned that an expression of anger to a person really demonstrated caring enough to tell. This means that one cares enough to want to see remedial action take place so that a relationship can continue and grow. An expression of anger also demonstrates respect for the individual in question. This is so because in expressing anger one is investing emotion—

showing how one feels and saying in effect, "I respect you enough to want to share this part of myself with you." This kind of expression also shows considerable confidence in the strength of the relationship. The feeling here is that the relationship is important and strong enough to withstand bumps in the road. It will not come irreparably apart at the first gust of strong feelings. If anything, it will be strengthened as a result of increased understanding between the people involved as well as the increased feelings of reality that always follow clearing of the air. If a relationship is destroyed by a show of anger, then there's an excellent chance that it was a sick, destructive affair and that all parties are better off for its termination.

Anger Doesn't Kill

This seems obvious, but it isn't to many people; anger doesn't kill healthy relationships, and it certainly does not kill people. If anything, denied anger, perverting and twisting, results in the killing of relationships and people, too. Many "don't-make-wavers" are afraid that anger kills because they think that it kills love—and how can one live without love? The "love" they speak of is invariably highly neurotic and is, as a matter of fact, impossible to live with. Anger of course does make waves and kills the neurotic kind of "love" that depends on a show of 100 percent complete harmony. But this isn't love at all; it is neurotic dependency and only confused with love. Feeling anger and exchanging angry feelings strengthen true love and are actually life-affirming. I am reminded of the pushcart section on the Lower East Side of New York and the jewelry stands in the Bowery Exchange in New York. Time and again I have heard real, passionate arguing, bargaining, as well as the exchange of real angry feelings. But I have never seen anyone raise a hand to anyone else. People sound off their anger, but they don't hurt one another. I know some of the men in the Bowery Exchange, and at times they get very competitive and angry with one another. But they are close friends; they help one another and have had solid relationships extending over twenty-five years. By contrast, have you ever thought of controlled, ultrapolite generals who aren't angry at all but who quietly order the destruction of whole populations?

It isn't anger that kills; people kill—people who are often completely divorced from all their feelings, especially warm human ones that would give them the wherewithal to empathize with their fellows.

Drop Dead!

When a mother says, "Drop dead!" to her child, she means drop dead for a little while only. This is another way of saying, "Drop dead for as long as my anger lasts, which is about two seconds." This *finite* characteristic of anger is so important that I want to stress it here under a separate heading.

Now is not forever! Being angry *now* does not mean being angry forever *if*—and this is a big *if*—*if* the anger is felt, accepted, and not relegated to the slush fund. Slush-fund anger can go on and on and on and on, but this is not true of anger truly experienced as anger. When one feels it—for real—the reaction is always finite. It does not last—it passes—it is over with!

When a mother says, "Drop dead!" of course she does not mean drop dead at all. She means, "I am very angry for this moment because I am very displeased with you." More often than not, her anger is based on fear—fear that her child will get hurt, lost, killed, and so on. These very strong words are extremely useful because (1) they serve to express her angry feelings to herself and to her child; (2) they are indicative of how much she really does care; (3) their strength (the strength of her response) ensures a fast dissipation and end of her angry feelings, which will be replaced by better understanding and the expression of much love.

Forgive and Forget

A corollary of the finite quality of anger is the ability to forgive and to forget. One cannot forgive and forget with a slush fund on one's back. Anger must be experienced, dissipated, and ended for forgiving and forgetting to take place. *Forgiving and forgetting* are extremely important to mental health and to healthy relationships. Long-standing grudges are extremely corrosive and damaging to the self. They are ultimately accompanied by mild to severe paranoid states, and destroy all possibility of fruitful relationships. An inability to forgive and to forget (wrongdoings and personal hurts) guarantees a source of perpetual pain and chronic misery. Our pushcart peddlers know how to sound off, how to forgive and to forget, and how to go on to conduct business, friendships, and life as usual.

With or Without Justice

Again and again people ask, "I was right, wasn't I? It was right to get angry, wasn't it?" Asking whether or not anger is justified is especially common with former "don't-make-wavers" who are just beginning to make waves.

Justice or justification simply has no bearing on the angry issue. Getting angry is neither right nor wrong. People who seek justification are attempting to rationalize or to excuse their anger because they don't quite accept it. Getting angry, like getting hungry, is a human phenomenon, and neither needs an excuse for being. If someone is hungry, he is hungry, and the fact that he has just eaten does not mitigate his hunger. The same is true of anger. If he is angry, he is angry regardless of any right or wrong issue involved. There is simply no right or wrong or moral equivocation here.

If there is a misunderstanding or irritation or frustration, then there is no justification or lack of justification for it We can always cite as many reasons or factors to justify a particular angry feeling or act as we can to declare it unjustified. It all depends on the point of view and the particular frame of reference. *But* no amount of justifying or intellectualization will clear the air and repair communications as will simple expressions of anger. Once anger is felt, it is felt—regardless of the state of justice in which it occurs. Once it is felt through, expressed, and exchanged—unfettered and undiluted by excuses for being—*then* its causes and the elucidation thereof may be valuable in terms of insight regarding one's relating or the particular relationship involved.

Appropriate and Inappropriate

Anger seems inappropriate only when we don't understand it. If it is appropriate to the situation on hand, we usually understand it and usually judge it to be appropriate. When its intensity appears to be proportionate to the stimulus, we usually deem it as appropriate. When there is no apparent reason for anger or when it seems much more intense than a situation calls for, then we usually look upon it as disproportionate or inappropriate. However, anger is always appropriate. It may be appropriate to a source that is mysterious or unknown to the observer, but in terms of that source, it is appropriate. Once that source is disclosed, then anger appears appropriate to the observer, too. This is true of all human emotional responses. They may seem to be irrational in terms we are all acquainted with and call rational. But all responses, however irrational, do have a rationale or meaning—however hidden or complicated that meaning may be. A schizophrenic patient may in our terms of making sense make no sense when he talks. But if we spend great effort and time to "learn his language," a special kind of logic will usually come to light.

Anger that seems inappropriate or disproportionate to a given situation is very often hooked to past, hidden, slush-fund sources. Great "inappropriate-looking" rages are often due to some old, raw sore spot that is inadvertently grated by a seemingly small present-day incident. Karen Horney, in her various works, brilliantly described reactions to hurt pride and thwarted claims.

Angry reactions at hurt pride can be quite obscure. For example, there are some people who get angry because they let themselves go and dare to love. This goes against the pride invested in *not capitulating and loving.* The result may be loving and feeling good and feeling angry all at the same time. Neurotic pride invariably covers up great feelings of inadequacy and self-hate. Any hurt to that pride threatens a denouement and the possibility of facing one's hated self. Being stripped by anyone in this way, and thus being terribly humiliated, evokes not only rage but also breaks open a storehouse of self-hate, which may also be converted to outer rage. I remember a man who nearly killed another man who jokingly asked if he was impotent. The second man had no idea that his question released in the first enormous self-hate and rage that had their basis in long-standing feelings of sexual inadequacy and possible impotency. The enraged man had always covered up his feelings with great pride invested in sexual conquests and prowess.

Dr. Horney describes thwarted neurotic claims as a source of intense anger. I must say that these reactions are exceedingly common; we see them very often in psychiatric treatment. People have desires; somehow neurotic people convert these desires to claims. "I would like this or that" becomes "You owe me this or that." When the claim is not fulfilled, rage ensues. Following is an example of a claim and reaction from my own practice and described in *The Winner's Notebook*.

My patient was a very shy physician. He and his wife were at a party where drinks and food were placed on a large center table. Guests were seated around the room and could help themselves when they desired. My patient got thirstier and thirstier but was too shy to get up and get a drink. On the way home he suddenly pulled the car to the curb and in great anger yelled at his wife, "You and your lousy friends—they wouldn't even give a guy a drink." What happened here? Dr. X had a desire for a drink, and because of his shyness, he wanted someone to get the drink for him. In this way he wouldn't have to get up, and he wouldn't have come face to face with his shy problem. This desire became a claim. His hosts owed him: (1) knowledge that he did not want to get up; (2) saving him from his problem; (3) the service of bringing him a drink. Since none of these debts were paid, he was enraged—especially because his pride was hurt and he had come face to face with a part of himself he hated and kept hidden. In terms of his neurosis his "disproportionate" anger was appropriate. His wife did not understand what it was all about—especially since the people at the party were his friends and not hers at all.

In this connection let me add that if someone really blasts you for what seems utterly inappropriate, listen carefully. You will probably learn a good deal about the person doing the blasting.

By the Sex

There is no sexual discrimination in anger. Members of both sexes are equally capable of getting angry and expressing anger. Yet some people have very confused ideas about this. Among those I've heard personally are the following:

Big angry displays are not feminine.

Big angry displays are only feminine and are not masculine.

Gentlemen simply don't show anger.

Ladies must not get angry at gentlemen.

Gentlemen must not get angry at ladies.

Very loud angry displays are evidence of homosexuality.

Of course all this is patent nonsense. Members of both sexes get equally angry, are equally expressive, and get angry at members of the same or of the other sex.

By Age

Anger is not the exclusive province of a particular age group. Age does not necessarily bring wisdom, nor does wisdom bring a cessation to angry feelings or to their expression. In vital people, who feel for themselves and their fellows, anger will exist regardless of age. Anger is certainly a feeling common to adults and children of all ages. Yet some parents seen to equate "goodness in children" with a lack of anger. They also expect their children somehow to control this emotion more than adults do. Healthy children with loads of vitality have a good range and capacity for all feelings including anger. Unlike adults they have developed neither the neurological systems nor the duplicitous devices necessary for "control." Despite a rather disturbed environment many children somehow retain the capacity to feel and to transmit both anger and love.

Warm, Cold, and In-Between

The subject here is quality. There are many subtle differences and nuances in the quality of anger. There are many in-betweens and combinations, but if we discuss the extreme poles—warm and cold—I think we will adequately cover ample ground.

Warm anger is the healthy stuff we spoke of in defining anger. With warm anger there is little or no time lapse between stimulus and feeling—between feeling it and expressing it. The expression of anger is warm, open, direct, and easy to understand. This is so because its principal purpose is to communicate how one feels and to make the other person aware of a need for greater understanding. Words and intensity may be strong, but they are usually appropriate to the issue in question, and there is little or no evidence of vindictiveness, sadism, or vengeful purpose. There is ample confidence and respect for the other person and what he feels. This is demonstrated by a willingness to stay put and to receive his affective message openly. Thus in warm anger there is always a warm emotional exchange. Words and gestures are not used flippantly or casually; they are not used as dissection tools either. Strong language is the poetry of anger, and we should expect poetry. But poetry does not include sarcastic biting, tearing, and stabbing. Obviously, the words and expressions will vary from culture to culture and from background to background (educational, familial, etc.). But they will always be words and will in no way involve physical force, coercion, or brutality. All expressions of warm anger will be short, finite; they will not go on and on and become chronic. There will be no grudge-carrying or slush accumulations. Angry feelings will be short-lived—finished and over with—and will be followed by forgiving and forgetting if appropriate. The expression of warm anger will have a cleansing effect on the relationship. It will clear the air of cobwebs of confusion, hurt feelings, and misunderstandings. There will always be at least two people involved, and they will always feel better for having had their exchange. Their mutual respect will have increased, and their mutual frame of reference (common ground) will be extended so that better and further understanding will ensue. Thus angry responses in the future will probably be reduced in frequency and intensity. There will be increased confidence and close-ness in the relationship. Protagonists will have demonstrated that they care enough to feel and to invest and to exchange feelings, thus substantiating that warm anger's closest relative is love.

Cold anger is often an internalized, unexpressed (through regular means), autistic slush-fund product, in which there is usually aberrated awareness. Any expression that takes place is accomplished through poisons. The purpose of any expression is too often vindictive triumph and the creation of sadistic pain. There is no interest in augmenting mutual under-standing, and no constructive emotional exchange takes place as one loses the ability to invest emotions in hostility. For our purpose here, we may say that this hostility is a state of sullen, chronic, corrosive anger sustained beyond ordinary self-limiting boundaries and always connected to old hates and slush. Cold anger feeds upon itself and its victim and tends to become more and more grotesque. It undermines self-esteem and one's confidence in others and the ability to relate to them. Differences grow and grow as it feeds paranoid feelings, cynicism, bitterness, and hopelessness. Any satisfaction derived from outward manifestation is almost always connected to one or another form of vindictive triumph. This kind of "gloating" satisfaction is usually short-lived and requires larger and larger sadistic enterprises in order to be felt at all.

These gloating experiences always leave their victims feeling still more hopeless, depressed, and empty, and augment the feeling of inner deadness.

Cold anger is used in the service of magnifying faults and destroying relationships. It is, therefore, a powerful influence in isolating and encapsulating one from one's fellows and ultimately from oneself. This takes place as one loses the ability to invest emotions in others—blocked largely by a frozen tundra of slush—and to experience other feelings. In short, the victim becomes a prisoner of his rage, trapped in a frozen waste, preoccupied with slush, leaving no energy, time, or room for other feelings. As time goes on, he loses the ability to extricate himself and to reach out and touch his fellows. Cold anger is obviously the antithesis and enemy of love.

All or Nothing

I believe that you feel either all your feelings or eventually none at all. You cannot select which feelings you will feel and which you won't. People attempt to do this in order to admit only those feelings that fit in with the particular ways in which they want to see themselves. This is of course especially true of "nice guys." They pay a very large price for this attempted selection. I say "attempted" because it never really works. They may think it works, but the slush fund grows and grows, and poisons are produced that are inevitably very destructive. Perverted anger is also converted to anxiety, which produces myriad defenses or symptoms comprising destructive neurosis and even psychosis. But the price paid in terms of other feelings is even greater. The fact is that you simply can't have one feeling without the other. Negate anger and you must also negate love. Love requires a real self and a real exchange between real selves. People who are not themselves, who are acting a part, cannot make a real exchange. They can only act. Additionally, when the air is not cleared, however peaceful the climate looks, the blocks and barriers to exchange become insurmountable, making feelings of love (caring about the other individual at least as much as one cares about one's self) impossible. But it is more than this, too.

When we use energy to put down anger, we must also continue to expend energy to keep it down—to keep guard, as it were. This use of energy depletes the free flow and tapping of energy needed to feel other feelings. It is as if we use a major part of ourselves to sit on a particular feeling. If we sit, we can't stand up to experience other feelings. Sitting on a feeling effects a freeze-up, which gradually encroaches on all feelings, causing a paralysis of feelings and even obliteration. This energy tie-up and freeze-up must be freed and melted so that the free feel and expression of all feelings can take place. I remember a particularly "sweet-mannered" woman who came to see me in a consultation. Despite her smiles and gentle manner, her chief complaint was that she simply felt nothing, not even for her children. She wanted to "feel again." She readily admitted to sitting on anger for years. She did not know that in effect she had successfully converted all her feelings to an iceberg, which now needed thawing.

Anger and love and the feeling of both do not operate in separate compartments or in separate people. We cannot reject one and hope to experience the other. An insult to one will invariably produce repercussions in the other. Respect, acceptance, and the giving of full life to one feeling is necessary for full development and experience of the others. I have a patient who recently told me, "As soon as the anger got out, I became aware of so many things—of feeling love and living and noticing wild flowers again."

The Big Blow-Up

Big blow-ups are really the accumulated results of re-pressed potential small air-clearing blow-ups. People often wait and wait to get things off their chest—and then finally approach the time of the big blow-up with great trepidation Unfortunately, they have to prime the emotional pump before they get going. Some of the same people use anger as the pushing force in aggressive moves. They must get very angry before they can act and their actions are destructively aggressive rather than healthily self-assertive. Much of the energy of the big blow-up is derived from distortions and exaggerations that have taken place during the long waiting period. Most relationships survive the big blow-up, which usually effectively clears the air. As a matter of fact, it often puts a formerly stagnant and paralyzed relationship back on the road to constructive movement. Small angry encounters, however, remain the best weapon against the stagnation of unexchanged feelings. Small blow-ups are straighter, less distorted, better hooked into reality, less traumatic, and more thorough in their house-cleaning effects. This is so because the time lapse between stimulus and response is shorter. Do try to not avoid small blow-ups.

To Be Angry and to Be Mad

Madness and anger have been confused for years. As I mentioned earlier, this is so largely because angry feelings are seen as loss of control or too much involvement or as a threat to being loved—all the antitheses of one's unrealistic aspirations. To feel and to express anger healthily is actually the antithesis of madness. It may not fit in with a saintly image, but a saintly image hardly functions in behalf of one's health. Healthy angry feelings and a healthy outlet for those feelings are the real antidote for slush and poison. Healthy emotional expression prevents the build-up of extraordinary pressures that are so deleterious to physical and mental health. The healthy and appropriate feel and expression of human emotions and especially anger make for an enormous contribution to mental health. This is in fact so true that many psychiatrists, through observation of how a patient handles anger, can assess his state of mental health—with considerable accuracy. The ways, the depths, the amplitude of angry feelings and response often provide a key to a patient's health and sickness as well as much information concerning his particular neurotic processes and how they work. If an individual "gets mad" now and then, he is certainly not "going mad" by any means. He may, in fact, be amassing important assets against madness.

While the Storm
Blows

It is sometimes very useful to retrace steps and to understand where particular angry responses came from—that is, what they are about. This can lead to much insight, that is, self-understanding and growth. But don't attempt to stop an angry response to do this. It will sit there stymied and serve as a block to any understanding. It is likewise useless to try to do this in the middle of the storm. To do so will only add confusion and may also "spoil" the storm. The best reexaminations—the most useful and constructive—are made after the storm is over. The air is now cleared. One feels unburdened and lighter. One has a sense of relief, openness, calm, and receptivity. This is the best time and climate for examination and evaluation. Incidentally, some of the most valuable questions to ask are those pertaining to the anger itself:

"Did I feel and get angry warmly, fully, and openly without guilt and recriminations?" "Did I give the other fellow a chance to unburden himself?" But more about questions in Part 5.

Angry Psychiatrists

Hostile psychiatrists are useless and even dangerous. But the same is also true of psychiatrists who do not get angry. They either have not worked out their own angry problems or they are putting on a rigid, stilted, professional act. God save the patient from the doctor who pushes buttons and turns parts of himself off when he acts in "a professional capacity." The psychiatrist above all must have all of himself available to himself if he is to use the most exquisite instrument there is in healing the patient. This instrument is himself, and he cannot cut parts of himself out—or anesthetize parts. I am very grateful because my own analyst was the same whole man in the office and out of the office. Sometimes he was an angry man. All his emotions were available to him, and he was *completely* (all of him—not selective parts) tuned in to our relationship and helping me. The psychiatrist who is aware of his angry feelings will not inadvertently and unconsciously use the patient as a foil for his own slush. The psychiatrist who is well analyzed and tuned into himself will be there to help the patient and not to exploit him. He will have few or no blind spots—and will see the patient in all his ramifications. There are times when a psychiatrist feels anger and irritation at a patient before he knows why. This open admission of anger in himself is a signal that something may be happening that neither the patient nor he is consciously aware of. It often leads to recognition of unconscious, subtle hostility and manipulations on the part of the patient. This kind of "discovery" can be used to extend the patient's knowledge of himself in the service of getting well.

In actuality, most well-analyzed psychiatrists do not get angry at a patient as much as they get angry and irritated at a patient's manifestations of neurosis and destructiveness. This does not mean that they reject either the patient or his symptoms. Quite the contrary, they accept the patient in his entirety—much more than the patient himself does—including the patient's neurosis. Part of this respect and acceptance may include angry feelings. *Remember,* angry feelings are the antithesis of rejection. *Remember,* healthy angry feelings are synonymous with respect, confidence, and caring. Deep down both the patient and doctor will know and appreciate this.

I remember making rounds in a very disturbed ward of a state hospital. A patient came up to me and without a word spit in my face. I didn't put on an act and smile sweetly, nor did I ignore his gesture. This would have been dishonest and disrespectful, as well as a phony attempt to be other than human. He did this because, among other things, he felt angry and this was his way of telling me. This made me very angry, and I let him in on my anger in no uncertain terms. The air was cleared. Among other things, he felt more secure because I told him what I would and would not take, thus establishing realistic limits of behavior which he could recognize and use. He had also tested my honesty—and I passed. We later shook hands and became friends. He knew that I respected him, and his trust in me was sufficiently established so that he told me of many of his "gripes" and dissatisfactions, making a therapeutic and progressive relationship possible.

Let me say that deep down everybody appreciates a show of real honest-to-goodness feelings. This is particularly true of very disturbed people who have lost touch with their own feelings and who are seeking their way back. They are the first to recognize saccharin, phoniness, or an attempt at control. They are also the first to recognize the real thing and an honest person who deals with them on an honest feeling level.

TAKING A CHANCE
ON ANGER

This section consists of 103 questions designed as an exercise to open up and to extend angry and loving ability.

Knowing how we pervert and how we twist anger and knowing about angry realities and how we personally react can be very helpful in taking a chance on anger, on love, and on health.

Questions

1. Are you aware that taking a chance on feeling angry and expressing anger get easier and easier? It may be difficult at first but gets much easier as healthy habits are established. Remember that you are working in the service of healthier and happier communication with yourself and others. Getting used to a change in *status quo* takes time. We humans are terribly afraid of the unfamiliar, even when the unfamiliar is pure health. Getting used to healthy anger takes time and practice.

2. Have you ever experienced the good, clean feeling that comes after expressing anger, as well as the increased self-esteem and the feel of real peace with one's self and others?

3. Are you solidly aware that the purpose of warm, healthy anger is to deliver an affective (emotional) message in order to clear the air and to make corrections and reparations if necessary?

4. Are you solidly aware that the ultimate effects of healthy angry displays are improved communications and better relating?

5. Are you aware that poisons are reversible and that much hope exists? People can change if they really so desire. Motivation is all-important.

6. When was the last time you got solidly angry? Did the world cave in?

7. Do you deprive your friends of your whole self, or do you give them the benefit of your anger and all your feelings—honestly, as they really are?

8. Do you have real friends, or have your friendships been based on a "don't-make-waves" basis?

9. Do you know any "pushcart dealers"—who are loud, angry, warm, and voluble, but who don't hurt one another and remain good friends?

10. Do you sound off, or do you keep angry secrets?

11. Do you lump all anger together, or do you know the differences in intensity and kinds of anger?

12. Do you give your anger full free rein and expression, unafraid of "losing control," or do you cut it short—stump it—before it really gets going?

13. Do you avoid little blow-ups until you face a much-dreaded major blow-up?

14. Are you fully aware that anger is not the same as sustained hostility and hatred?

15. Are you aware that anger is closely linked to love and that you can and usually do get angry at people you love? Love and anger are not mutually exclusive. You can get deeply angry at people and love them enough so that you want the very best of all things for them.

16. Are you aware that the biggest dangers are not feeling and not knowing what we feel? Accepting anger equals feeling equals knowing who and what we are.

17. Do you know that this book could have as accurately been called *The Love Book*?

18. What is wrong with this statement: "If I get angry, she won't like me"? If you are angry but don't show it and she likes "you," will she like you or your act? If she likes "acts," how healthy can she and your relationship be?

19. Do you get angry only when you are "right" and "justified"? Do you therefore always try to justify your anger, or do you instead get angry and then really try to find out what it is all about?

20. Do you get angry only when it is "safe"—for example, with people you know are too self-effacing to dish it back; at people who you know surely, absolutely surely, love you; when you are in a car, anonymous among other anonymous "victims"?

21. Do you take full responsibility for yourself, your feelings, and your anger? Or do you substitute guilt and apology for responsibility and acceptance? Are you aware that when you are fully responsible for an expression of how you feel, you are truly identifying yourself?

22. Are you an angelic phony or are you anesthetized? If you never get angry, you must be either one or the other or suffering from severe brain damage.

23. The reasons for anger or the stimuli that touch off anger are multiple, varied, complex, and individual, but the important fact is that they are always present— so, do you get angry?

24 Are you aware that healthy anger functions in the service of real closeness?

25. Isn't the goal a world without violence rather than a world without anger?

26. Do you know emotional half-wits—people who attempt to feel only "the right feelings"?

27. Have you ever traced an attack of anxiety down and back to angry feelings that you were perverting, thus preventing the accumulation of slush and the manufacture of poisons? In doing this you have revealed to yourself what you really feel in pure form and have moved toward greater self and health.

28. When people ask you, "Am I right to be angry?" have you thought of asking them, "Am I right to be thirsty?" Of course if they ask you about actual issues and your opinion, this is something else. But don't be sucked into helping them rationalize a basic human emotion.

29. Do you know that it is entirely possible to get angry at someone to whom you are grateful? These are not contradictory or hypocritical feelings, nor is anger evidence of being an ingrate. You can be grateful to a person because of certain matters and angry at the same person in response to other matters.

30. Do you know that often the depth of angry feelings cannot exceed the depth of loving, tender feelings toward a particular person?

31. What is your time lapse between getting angry and feeling angry and between feeling anger and showing anger? Are you shortening the lapse and getting healthier?

32. Do you get angry *straight* so that it is completely discernible?

33. How are your forgiving-and-forgetting mechanisms? If they are in good order, chances are that your angry outlook is good enough for you to have warm, healthy, cleansing angry responses.

34. Are you caught in the big swindle—being liked at any cost to yourself, to your synthetic friends, and to your relationships?

35. Are you open to an accepting of the possibility of having all kinds of feelings and responses?

36. Do you recognize any perversions and poisons as your very own?

37. What do you estimate is the depth of your slush fund?

38. Are you aware that your anger will not kill anyone and that no one's anger will kill you?

39. Are you afraid of loud voices? Stick around and listen to them for a while. Try out your own, O.K.?

40. Are you afraid to speak up and to cut the time lapse? Take a chance and give yourself a chance!

41. Do you remember that anger is not forever? Unlike slush, it is finite?

42. Are you aware that expressing anger reduces anger and makes angry reactions shorter? This seems obvious, but many people operate as if it weren't so.

43. Are you aware that psychiatrists and psychoanalysts are people and, like all people, get angry if they are healthy—and for real?

44. Was there freedom of emotional expression in your parents' house? If so, then you are fortunate indeed.

45. Are you aware that people can feel loving and make love after a "fight" because an emotional traffic jam has been cleared?

46. Do you know that group therapy can be very valuable for angry problems, provided the members of the group are chosen with great care by an expert therapist?

47. If you cannot extricate yourself from the slush-fund morass, are you wise enough to seek expert professional help? This means going to a psychiatrist who is a graduate of a psychoanalytic institute recognized by either The American Academy of Psychoanalysis or The American Psychoanalytic Association.

48. Are you aware that hostility can be expressed in very subtle thoughts as well as blatant fantasies? I remember a patient who was unaware of his hostility toward his wife. When he felt particularly hostile, he would worry about her safety. "Wonder if she got hit by a car?" He had no idea that he worried because of his own hostile feelings and desire for punishment for her. On the other hand, a colleague of mine saw a man who had very blatant hostile fantasies but who also was unaware of his feelings. "Me angry—never! Fantasies? Well sometimes I have a funny one. I look out of my office window during the lunch hour. Loads of people pouring into the street. I picture myself at the window with a machine gun rat-ta-ta-ta pouring lead into them. Sometimes I picture a lion or a tiger loose among them."

49. Are you aware that people who are accident-prone are full of self-hate and inadvertently seek the possibility of getting hurt? These people ski on slopes that are too steep for them; skate on ice that is too thin; climb mountains that are too high; race cars that are too fast, and walk in dark, dangerous places.

50. Do you get chronically depressed? How distant are you from your feelings?

51. How do you show your anger? Do you make ample use of your voice, gestures, strong language? Are you aware of the purpose of strong language?

52. "I just haven't been angry in years." Are you aware that this is the statement of a very angry man who is the probable owner of a large slush fund?

53. Do you always think of what to say later—when it is too late? If so, how come?

54. When you get angry do you smile or laugh it off or go off to another room and cry? If so, how come?

55. Do you sit and sulk and eat yourself up?

56. Do you get caught in pride deadlocks? Can you try to break out early—to speak up and make a move? Are you aware that you and your pride do not operate on the same wave length? If you cater to your neurotic pride, you do not cater to your health and your true self.

57. Do you spend sleepless nights? If so, what is on your mind? Is it slush and poison that are keeping you awake? What are your thoughts at bedtime?

58. Are you sleeping your life away in an attempt to put your anger to sleep?

59. Are you aware that some people use perverted anger to get moving, instead of using real motivation and self-assertion? These people cannot make decisions or moves until they have accumulated enough energy from small slush-fund explosions to give them the push? "I was so mad I just had to do something."

60. Are you aware that perverted anger is one of the most destructive elements in sexual relationships? People who are angry and don't know it are in a poor position to be good lovers. Sexual activity is not always loving activity.

61. Do you know the difference between self-assertion and aggression? Self-assertion springs from self-esteem, the spontaneous ability to make a choice and to do something in one's behalf with no desire to hurt others. Aggression is a compulsive act designed "to put someone else down." Its principal energy is derived from slush, and its imagined gain is based on the attempted domination of others.

62. Are you aware that sympathy and empathy for a person do not preclude anger at him?

63. Do "good mothers" get angry at their children, and do "good children" get angry at their mothers? Contrary to neurotic opinion, children that get angry and freely express their anger can also respect their parents.

64. Would children rather be yelled at or ignored?

65. When you are angry, how do you use your mouth—to overeat or to speak up?

66. How many grudges comprise a back-breaking load?

67. Are you aware that "slush-fund people" often use sex as an aggressive act?

68. Have you and your wife talked angrily to each other in the last six months? Lovingly? Have you talked?

69. Do you attempt to wash away and freeze anger with ice-cold showers?

70. Do you encourage your children to express themselves—in all their feelings—or do you insist on more control than you yourself are capable of?

71. Do you steer clear of controversial discussions because you are afraid that strong feelings may slip out?

72. Do you save anger for enemies only? Why aren't you as good to your friends?

73. Do you have any "friends" who sweetly, smilingly, sneakily slip you hostile barbs of which they are seemingly unaware? Have you considered letting them in on their own secret—by telling them?

74. Do your jaw and face hurt because you keep your teeth clenched? If so, what are you trying to keep from saying?

75. Have you ever told a compulsive joker or a chronic bore that you are bored?

76. Do you speak up when you feel the yen? How is your digestion? Do you sleep well?

77. Do you tell people how you feel by mail, over the telephone, or face to face?

78. When is the last time you have had a bad headache? Have you considered the possibility that you were angry and didn't know it? Have you tried to trace it back? Did anything happen that could have possibly irritated you?

79. Are you afraid to speak up because you may "hurt" the other fellow? Do you want to hurt him, or do you want to tell him of your displeasure? If you tell him of your displeasure and he gets hurt, do you realize that this is his problem and not yours? Isn't it enough to take responsibility for yourself? Isn't it your responsibility not to cheat either of you out of sharing the communication between you? Are you afraid he will hurt you? Do you think you are perfect and perfectly lovable and incapable of irritating the next fellow? Are you afraid that you will get even angrier at him? Is it possible that neither you nor he nor your relationship is as fragile as you thought and that all will survive in real, worthwhile survival terms?

80. Do you make love after a "fight" is really over and done with and make good love because you really feel love? Or do you have sex after a fight whether you feel like it or not, whether the angry feelings are gone or not—as a mechanical, automatic process to get rid of anger as soon as possible? Do you realize that the sun can set on a lovers' quarrel—that lovers can go on being angry—without sex as an attempted communications panacea—for a sustained period of time? Are you aware that there is a difference between sustained anger that is felt and communicated and anger that is sustained through relegation to the slush fund—which is neither felt nor communicated but eventually twisted to poisons? So, are you aware of the difference between sex used to sweep anger under the bed and sex used to express love *after* anger has really been expressed and has passed?

81. Are you a perpetual peacemaker, forcing people directly or through manipulations ("How much I suffer when you fight") to shake hands when they are not ready to? Or do you allow people to get it off their chest—to clear the air so that they can become even better friends? Are you aware that real peace and real friendship preclude violence and dishonesty but include the feeling and transmission of displeasure as well as pleasure?

82. Are you afraid of getting close to people because you may get "hurt"? Is this possibly the result of your wanting to "hurt" others? If so, this can have the snowball effect of perverting what started out as a little anger. Help by an expert may be indicated.

83. When you have a heart-to-heart talk with a friend or relative, is it always in purely intellectual, calm, cool, collected terms? Is it ever warm, voluble, dramatic?

84. What kind of toys do you buy your children? I know a very "peace-loving, nice, nice man" who bought his children (exclusively) bows and arrows, darts, guns, etc. When this was pointed out to him, he switched to soldiers, tanks, and bazookas. He understood with his head, but it took a long time to work out his angry feelings and to understand with his heart. Eventually he stopped his unconscious identification with aggression.

85. Are you a nice, nice guy who plays all games to "beat" the other fellow? Or are you a not-so-nice guy who likes to win but mainly plays to have fun?

86. Are you a gentle, nice, peace-loving lady who attacks food, plunging knife and fork in and stabbing away as if at an enemy? Does this tend to occur after certain little discussions with certain people? Are you aware of what your table activity is like? How is your weight lately? What is the weight of slush?

87. Does your little boy try and try again to provoke you? How come he is so provocative? What is he trying to perk up in you? Is he asking you for limits within which he can behave? Is he asking you for a healthy angry response so as to make sure you are after all warm, vital, human? Are you aware of how hard it is to live with a sweet, saintly, always tranquil, highly intellectualizing (here using words rather than feelings) mother—when a person is young, vibrant, strong-feeling, and has a need to exchange the feelings? Have you thought about the extraordinary amount of guilt "sweet" mothers seem to provoke in their children? Could this guilt be a manipulative tool—to get the children to do their bidding without telling them and telling them angrily, if necessary?

88. Did your parents ever sound off at you in no uncertain terms? Do you love them the less for this? I've never run into anyone who had a grudge against his parents for having been honestly angry with him and having shown it. Vindictive feelings toward parents are usually born of complicated neurotic relating factors. Many are connected to feeling that parents were duplicitous, dishonest, and sneakily manipulative and exploitative. Children do not love parents for conning them with false sweetness. They love them for the real love they receive, and one way this is felt is through the expression of honest, healthy feelings.

89. Are you aware that constipation (bowels) is often a concomitant of constipated emotions and tightness, especially in people who attempt to control and to keep all angry feelings under wraps?

90. Are there genuinely nice, sweet people in this world? Yes, absolutely yes, and they get angry as often as you and I. They must—otherwise they would be full of vindictive feelings and slush, which would prevent *genuine sweetness*.

91. Do you know any phony, sweet, vindictive people? I remember one woman I saw in a consultation for the city. She couldn't have been "sweeter" in manner. She "just never got angry." She had no idea why she did it, but "something just got touched off in me and the next thing it was happening like I wasn't there to stop it." She had thrown a bottle of carbolic acid into a neighbor's eyes, blinding her and scarring her for life. It was her slush fund that got touched off—and the fact that she hadn't been in touch with her anger for years.

92. Do you pay close attention to your child when he is delivering an affective message? Do you give him ample leeway and time to deliver the whole message? Does he have as much of your love, attention, and receptivity as when he delivers a sweet (truly sweet) message?

93. Are you overly drawn to fights? Sadistic people? Violent movies? How come? What is the state of your regular angry outlets—like telling people when you are angry?

94. Do you know anyone who is in psychiatric treatment, who is trying to change? Does he get angry now and then even though he never used to? Are you receptive—do you give him a chance? Or are you shocked, disappointed, and rejecting? I have seen very sick people begin to change and get well and have watched friends and relatives fight this change and curse the psychiatrist for it. People unfortunately are terribly afraid of any change in *status quo* even when it means greater health. This is especially true of a person whose own neurosis is in any way threatened—which is often the case of relatives of patients. Quite often the *relatives* have greater problems than the *patients*.

95. Have you discovered any sweet private little poisons of your own that I have not mentioned? Good—then you have already started the work of untwisting.

96. Do you smoke a pipe peacefully or do you chew it into pieces? Observe men who smoke cigars. Some actually smoke it. Others chew it up in repressed rage.

97. Are you absolutely sure that I am not suggesting synthetic shows of anger? Please be certain that I am against "angry acts." There is no point in putting on an act. The constructive thing to do is to listen in on one's self in order to become aware of feelings of anger.

98. Is it possible that the present generation of young people are not "angrier," but rather closer to their feelings, less stilted, freer—which is a credit to their parents and evidence of progress, however disturbing to some people?

99. When you are very angry do you go into a closet or into the bathroom and yell? It would be better if you could be more open about your feelings. But being open and expressive to yourself—and thus doing something to get relief—are certainly worthwhile.

100. Can you get angry about an issue, find out that your anger was disproportionate—a product of slush, admit it—take responsibility, apologize appropriately without underlying saccharine motivation? Then your direction is certainly a constructive one.

101. Did someone ever say to you, "You know something—I really like the way you look when you get angry"? It is entirely possible that he really meant it. He is responding to genuine and honest feeling and to your showing that feeling—for which there is really no substitute.

102. When your mother and father got genuinely and honestly angry with you was this followed by vindictive deprivation and rejection? I doubt it. Chances are that it went on concomitantly with love—and an honest demonstration of that love followed.

103. How about it? What is *your* angry self-evaluation? Are you growing? Are you taking a chance—on anger, on feeling, on loving, on being yourself—on living?

THEODORE ISAAC RUBIN, M.D., is a psychiatrist and former president of the American Institute for Psychoanalysis. Dr. Rubin is the author of twenty-five books, including *Lisa and David/Jordi*, *The Winner's Notebook*, *Compassion and Self-Hate*, and *Lisa and David Today*. He lives in New York City.